PE4life

Developing and Promoting
Quality Physical Education

Human Kinetics

Library of Congress Cataloging-in-Publication Data

PE4life
   PE4life : developing and promoting quality physical education / PE4life.
       p. cm.
   Includes bibliographical references.
   ISBN-13: 978-0-7360-5778-3 (soft cover : alk. paper)
   ISBN-10: 0-7360-5778-1 (soft cover : alk. paper)   1. Physical education for children--Study and teaching--United States. 2.
Physical education for children--Curricula--United States. I. Human Kinetics (Organization). II. Title. III. Title: PEforlife.
   GV443.P383 2007
   613.7'042--dc22
                                        2006025739

ISBN-10: 0-7360-5778-1
ISBN-13: 978-0-7360-5778-3

Consultants: Brenda VanLengen and Phil Lawler; **Acquisitions Editor:** Scott Wikgren; **Managing Editor:** Kathleen Bernard; **Copyeditor:** Annette Pierce; **Proofreader:** Erin Cler; **Permission Manager:** Carly Breeding; **Graphic Designer:** Fred Starbird; **Graphic Artist:** Dawn Sills; **Photo Manager:** Laura Fitch; **Cover Designer:** Keith Blomberg; **Photographer (cover):** © PE4life and © Human Kinetics (inset photos); **Photographer (interior):** © Human Kinetics and © PE4life (p. 11); **Art Manager:** Kelly Hendren; **Illustrator:** Lyndsey L. Groth (figure 1); Mic Greenberg (figure 8.1); and Argosy (figures 8.2 and 8.3); **Printer:** United Graphics

Printed in the United States of America   10 9 8 7 6 5 4 3 2 1

Human Kinetics
Web site: www.HumanKinetics.com

United States: Human Kinetics
P.O. Box 5076
Champaign, IL 61825-5076
800-747-4457
e-mail: humank@hkusa.com

Canada: Human Kinetics
475 Devonshire Road Unit 100
Windsor, ON N8Y 2L5
800-465-7301 (in Canada only)
e-mail: orders@hkcanada.com

Europe: Human Kinetics
107 Bradford Road
Stanningley
Leeds LS28 6AT, United Kingdom
+44 (0) 113 255 5665
e-mail: hk@hkeurope.com

Australia: Human Kinetics
57A Price Avenue
Lower Mitcham, South Australia 5062
08 8372 0999
e-mail: liaw@hkaustralia.com

New Zealand: Human Kinetics
Division of Sports Distributors NZ Ltd.
P.O. Box 300 226 Albany
North Shore City
Auckland
0064 9 448 1207
e-mail: info@humankinetics.co.nz

Contents

Foreword   v

Preface   vii

Introduction   ix

How to Use the DVD   xxiii

Part I   Building a PE4life Action Plan 1

Chapter **1**   Build Your Community-Based PE Team 3

Chapter **2**   Develop an Advocacy Strategy 11

Chapter **3**   Pinpoint Funding Opportunities 25

Chapter **4**   Get Equipped 33

Chapter **5**   Design Your PE4life Program 41

Chapter **6**   Develop a Plan to Assess Success 49

Chapter **7**   Learn to Troubleshoot and Overcome Roadblocks 57

Part II   Implementing the PE4life Program 65

Chapter **8**   Turn Your Plan Into a Curriculum 67

Chapter **9**   Implement Your Curriculum 79

Chapter **10**   Assess Your Students 89

Appendix A   Nutrition Resources   105

Appendix B   PE4life Resources   107

Appendix C   Sample Lesson Plans and Activities   119

Appendix D   Links to Physical Education Web Sites   155

Appendix E   References and Resources   157

About the Author   159

Foreword

During a long career as a physician and leading advocate for physical fitness, I've never seen the state of our kids' physical fitness worse than it is today.

In a country where more than 10 million children ages 6 to 17 are considered overweight and almost half of these are severely obese, it's more important than ever to educate young people about the importance of physical activity and a healthy lifestyle.

If we're going to halt the childhood obesity epidemic, and get our kids on a path toward physical fitness, one area that must improve drastically is our country's physical education system.

One of the best ways I've seen for doing that is the PE4life Program. I am very impressed with the PE4life model in general, and the PE4life Academies in particular. PE4life's "train the trainers" concept works.

Physical education in this country needs to move away from the traditional, competition-oriented team sports model and toward a health and wellness model emphasizing lifetime sports and physical activity. The PE4life approach to physical education does this. It is exactly what needs to happen if we are to have any hope of avoiding a medical disaster with this generation of children.

Kenneth H. Cooper, M.D., M.P.H.
Cooper Aerobics Center
Dallas, Texas
www.cooperaerobics.com

Preface

Changing the face of your physical education program isn't something that will just happen in your school—you must make it happen. And with a community-wide commitment to quality, daily physical education, you can make it happen.

This book and DVD package is designed to serve several purposes. If you have attended or will attend a PE4life Academy, this practical guide will supplement your experience and provide a step-by-step action plan to develop a PE4life Program in your school. To learn more about attending a PE4life Academy, please go to www.pe4life.org. A PE4life Program combines today's best practices in physical education to inspire and educate all students about the vital importance of lifetime physical activity and fitness. PE4life Programs incorporate cardiovascular fitness, muscular strength and endurance, and team building and adventure education within the curriculum; utilize technology and individualized student assessments; and encourage involvement within students' local health, medical, and business communities.

If you are a teacher in the field or a member of a curriculum committee who is seeking to upgrade your physical education program, you will find in this guide the tools that you need to get started. If you are a physical education director who is looking for quality in-service materials for your staff, you will find in this package an excellent combination of inspiration and concrete strategies. You can contact PE4life for possible in-service speakers. If you are an educational administrator who wants to learn more about quality physical education or implement your school's wellness policy, you will find here an excellent overview. And if you are a parent or other physical education advocate, you can obtain information from this package to help you promote quality physical education.

> "This training manual can really be used by all schools—whether you're just getting started or looking to further enhance a quality program with the resources and inspiration provided here."
>
> *Scott Topczewski,*
> *physical education instructor,*
> *Carl Sandburg Junior High School,*
> *Rolling Meadows, Illinois*

In addition, if you are a physical education educator at a college or university, you can use this resource to help prepare your students to become leaders at the schools where they end up teaching and where they can become effective advocates for quality physical education.

In part I of this resource we provide a comprehensive overview of why we need daily PE in schools and how you can make significant and dramatic improvements in your current system by developing a PE4life action plan. Here's a quick snapshot of the action steps that make up that plan:

- *Build your community-based PE team.* Identify and organize a group of people to pave the way for change within your district's PE program. Then identify long- and short-term goals to make it happen.

- *Develop an advocacy strategy.* Prepare yourself with the facts about why quality, daily PE is important to children's health and lifetime wellness. Cultivate partnerships to help you advocate for change in your community.

- *Pinpoint funding opportunities.* Determine how much each of your proposed changes will cost. Look within your school district for funding first. Then explore creative ways to find the funds that you need to support your program.

- *Get equipped.* Determine the best place to conduct your PE4life Program. Think about creative ways to use available space and then determine how you want to build out your space to accommodate new activities. Set priorities and a timeline for acquiring the equipment that you will need.

- *Design your PE4life Program.* Look for ways to embrace PE4life in your program to get all children active. Take a creative approach to existing sports activities by emphasizing movement, not athletics skills. Experiment with activities like kayaking, tennis, cross-country skiing, in-line skating, fly-fishing, juggling, and team-building exercises. Determine how you will stress the importance of lifetime physical activity.

- *Develop a plan to assess success.* Make it a priority to measure students' progress. Use heart rate monitors, fitness testing, and health assessments such as cholesterol screening to evaluate your students' overall health and wellness. Monitor progress over the course of days, weeks, and years.

- *Learn to troubleshoot and overcome negative perceptions.* Troublesome situations and outmoded beliefs concerning PE, funding issues, uncertainty in your community, and lack of physical space in your school can appear as you begin to put together your program. Think of ways to overcome these concerns.

In part II of this resource we provide more detailed strategies for implementing the PE4life action plan, with a focus on developing the curriculum, implementing the curriculum, and assessing your students. To provide additional support, we include more examples, resource lists, and Web links in the appendixes.

Also included in this package is a DVD that includes

- a 35-minute video of Phil Lawler leading a PE4life training session;
- a 10-minute video that promotes quality physical education;
- a 19-minute video featuring Dr. John Ratey talking about physical activity and brain research;
- handouts that promote quality physical education;
- reproducibles, worksheets, and other forms; and
- links to physical education Web sites.

For complete instructions on how to use the DVD, see pages xxiii-xxiv.

Introduction

Our Challenge

Almost 65 percent of adults in the United States are either overweight or obese. A report in the March 10, 2004, edition of the *Journal of the American Medical Association* cites statistics showing that 400,000 Americans died in 2000 because of lack of physical exercise and poor diet.

That's sad news. Even sadder is that our children are on pace to be significantly fatter than we are by the time they reach adulthood. The Centers for Disease Control and Prevention (CDC) reports that the number of children ages 6 through 11 who are overweight has increased over 300 percent over the past 25 years. The numbers are almost identical for teenagers.

We're in the middle of a childhood obesity epidemic, and the health implications are daunting. For example, until recently type 2 diabetes was considered an adult disease. In recent years, however, the incidence of the disease has increased dramatically in children and adolescents because more children are overweight. Dr. William J. Klish, professor of pediatrics at Baylor College of Medicine, noted that 27 percent of the children and adolescents at Texas Children's Hospital were found to have

type 2 diabetes in 2002, an astounding jump from less than 1 percent 20 years ago.

Making this picture even uglier is that while the physical fitness and health of our kids have been steadily declining, the number of PE classes in our schools has been dropping as well. This reduction has occurred despite the declarations of an array of experts who stress that children must engage in more physical activity if they are to avoid obesity and achieve optimal health. CDC research suggests that less than 10 percent of students attend physical education classes on a daily basis.

A variety of sociocultural developments over the past 25 years have combined to discourage a physically active lifestyle. In essence, our children are increasingly growing up in a culture that makes it easy to be sedentary. A

2006 report from the *International Journal of Pediatric Obesity* said that nearly half the children in North and South America will be overweight by 2010, with many other countries seeing increases in the number of overweight children as well. The consequences for them, and for the world as a whole, are staggering. The bottom line is that the children of America and the world need more physical activity. We're at a point in history where the need to teach our kids the benefits of a lifelong, physically active lifestyle has never been greater.

> "Children today have a shorter life expectancy than their parents for the first time in 100 years."
>
> *Dr. William J. Klish,*
> *professor of pediatrics,*
> *Baylor College of Medicine*

New technologies have allowed kids to be less active. New media (DVDs, computer games, cable and satellite television, and the like) have made sedentary activities more attractive. A 1999 national survey found that children ages 2 to 18 spent, on average, over four hours a day watching television and videos, playing video games, and using the computer. Television viewing accounts for most of that time, with 33 percent of kids watching more than three hours a day and 17 percent watching more than five hours a day.

States and school districts have devalued physical education, even in the face of growing problems with childhood obesity. The amount of time that students spend in physical education classes has decreased steadily over the past 25 years. Physical education has become a low priority for our nation's schools despite its proven benefits.

Increasingly concerned about safety, parents have restricted outside playtime for children, even in their own yards. Moreover, fear of injuries and lawsuits has led schools and recreation

How Did We Get to This Point?

Many factors have contributed to these frightening statistics. But among all these factors, physical inactivity stands out.

The Problem Starts With Toddlers

"There are really only two possibilities, reduced activity or increased intake. None of the dietary assessment data indicate that children are eating more," said John Reilly, leader of a study published in *Lancet* in January 2004. "Adolescents may be eating more but young children are eating less. A 3-year-old 25 years ago was eating 25 percent more than a 3-year-old today. But physical activity levels have dropped quite dramatically over the last 15 or 20 years."

A lack of physical activity remains the primary culprit through the teen years. Recent findings by researchers at San Diego State University and the School of Medicine at the University of California at San Diego found that the lack of physical activity was the most significant risk factor contributing to obesity in 11- to 15-year-olds.

Why the Big Drop in Physical Activity?

A variety of sociocultural developments over the past 25 years have combined to discourage physical activity.

Physical inactivity has contributed to the unprecedented epidemic of childhood obesity that is currently plaguing the United States, according to a year 2000 report to the president of the United States from the secretary of health and human services and the secretary of education.

At the most basic level of analysis, the childhood epidemic is caused by a poor balance between calories consumed and calories burned up. Although many people justifiably point their fingers at our youth's fast-food inclinations and "super size it" mentality—especially on the part of adolescents—research shows that the primary cause of the epidemic is that children today aren't getting enough exercise.

districts to tone down playground equipment to the point that the equipment provides only minimal exercise benefits.

Intramural sports programs in our public schools are going the way of the dinosaur as schools focus resources on sports participation for elite athletes at the expense of participation for all. Thus, students who are not good enough to make the elite teams and don't live in neighborhoods where pickup games occur are left out. Community investment in parks and recreation centers has also been inadequate. Thus, the lack of intramural programs and park and recreation programs leaves little opportunity for non-elite athletes to engage in physical activity after school and on weekends. Physical education, athletics, and recreation serve related but different purposes, and all are necessary to provide children and young adults the best chance to lead active, healthy lives.

Kids are walking and riding bicycles less than ever before. National transportation surveys have found that walking and bicycling by children ages 5 to 15 dropped 40 percent between 1977 and 1995. Parents and their cars are replacing walking and bicycling as the primary means of getting to school, as well as to after-school and summer activities.

Schools Will Eventually Be Held Accountable for Cutting PE and Other Means of Physical Activity

USA Today and other media have reported extensively on the dramatic increases in childhood obesity, including the contributing factors of lack of physical activity and exercise. Nowhere in this discussion of increasing obesity in children and adults and the lack of physical activity . . . has one of the major contributors been acknowledged. It's our culture of academic extremism—learning to read and write at all costs, including the cost of diminished physical activity

Recess, physical education, and play have all been reduced or eliminated while the length of the school day has been increased. Half-day kindergarten has been increased to full-day, and six-hour school days to seven, while the amount of homework in elementary school has also been increased. After-school programs that used to allow letting off of steam and developmentally normal play such as kickball games are now pressured to make sure homework is done and activities related to learning that will increase standardized test scores.

School systems control the physical activity of our children five days a week, nine months a year. Undeniably, parents have a great deal of control over what their children eat, which can lead to obesity. However, parents have no control over how much exercise their children are allowed in school or after-school programs. Our current education system has emphasized measurable academic data and standards. Height and weight measurements taken at the beginning of the school year and at the end can be compared to growth curve norms. School systems that have data showing increases above the norms should be held accountable.

For thousands of years, physical activity in children was a built-in developmental drive that the environment usually allowed for. Perhaps when school systems realize they are exposed to lawsuits by parents of overweight children . . . for denying the developmental necessity of physical activity, schools will make changes needed for allowing physical movement and active play.

Rich Scofield, founder, School-Age Notes

Why Is Quality, Daily Physical Education So Important?

In the United States more than 95 percent of 5- to 17-year-olds are enrolled in school, nearly 55 million kids in all. Schools are the only institutions that can reach nearly all of our kids.

Surveys indicate that more than 60 percent of children ages 9 through 13 do not participate in any organized physical activity during nonschool hours. For these kids, school-based physical education programs are the only place that they'll get any exercise and learn about important health and wellness issues that can positively affect the rest of their lives. A quality, daily physical education program that reaches all children is simply the most cost-effective delivery system in the country to combat our childhood obesity epidemic.

Note, however, that participation in physical education class still doesn't provide enough activity time in most cases. Various organizations have recommended that children get at least 60 minutes of physical activity each day, yet few physical education classes meet long enough to provide the full 60 minutes. And during physical education class, the focus must be not only on activity but also on instruction and learning.

Benefits of Quality, Daily Physical Education

Physical education helps students establish healthy lifestyle habits. It provides the skills that allow young people to take responsibility for their own health. Short term, participation

> "Americans have developed a 'drive everywhere' mentality. . . . We are teaching our children to get into the car, even for very short trips, and that is having a major health impact."
>
> *Lauren Marchetti, Pedestrian and Bicycle Information Center*

> "Children and teenagers today suffer from a lack of exercise. I would rather write a prescription for PE to combat this problem. Kids are too sedentary."
>
> *Dr. Norman Spack, Children's Hospital Boston*

in physical education class gives children the opportunity to exercise and become fit. Daily physical activity helps kids reduce stress, build energy, and gain confidence. Long term, physical education prepares children to take personal ownership of their health and wellness and improve their overall quality of life.

Improves Physical Health

Physical activity provides numerous benefits that lead to a high-quality life, including disease prevention.

Moreover, the connection between K–12 physical education and lifelong physical activity is clear. Studies show that people are more likely to develop and maintain healthy lifestyles when they learn about exercise and other healthy behaviors early in life.

A physically active lifestyle adopted early in life may continue into adulthood. Even among 3- and 4-year-olds, those who were less active tended to remain less active than most of their peers after age 3.

Enhances Mental Health

Research has shown that regular participation in physical activity during childhood and

Over 75 percent of U.S. children are not active for even 20 minutes a day, which is the minimum daily requirement. Many organizations recommend 60 minutes of activity a day for children.

adolescence reduces feelings of depression and anxiety. Studies have also revealed that physical activity and sports participation contribute to enhanced self-esteem.

Dr. John J. Ratey, a Harvard brain-research specialist, believes firmly that physical activity has a positive effect on the brain. In fact, he believes that exercise is fertilizer for the brain, calling it Miracle-Gro. Active kids are more confident, assertive, independent, and self-controlled.

Improves Academic Performance

Scientific evidence now supports the old idea of a "sound mind in a sound body." Several studies have shown a distinct relationship between academic achievement and physical fitness. In particular, recent research has determined that physical activity facilitates cognitive development. For example, in a 2002 California Department of Edu-

cation study, higher academic achievement was associated with higher levels of fitness. For more information, see Dr. John Ratey's video on physical activity and brain research that is included on this book's enclosed DVD.

Reaches At-Risk Students

Physical education provides an ideal mechanism to promote healthy choices and habits for those most in need, both physically and otherwise. For instance, a study conducted by Naperville (IL) High School's PE4life Academy found that high school students that took a fitness-based physical education course, in addition to a literacy class, improved their reading and comprehension scores by 1.4 years on a grade-level equivalency scale. This was a nearly 50 percent greater improvement than students who took the literacy class alone achieved.

> "The evidence shows that physical fitness is a stronger indicator than sports participation for self-esteem and relating to others. The kids feel better about themselves. The key concept is physical activity, not your skill level."
>
> *Don Hellison,*
> *professor of kinesiology,*
> *University of Illinois at Chicago*

Parents and Teachers Agree on the Value of Physical Education

- Eighty-one percent of teachers and 85 percent of parents favor requiring students to take physical education every day at every grade level.

- Eighty-seven percent of teachers and 88 percent of parents believe that school boards should not eliminate physical education for budgetary reasons.

- Eighty-seven percent of teachers and 77 percent of parents believe that schools should not eliminate physical education classes to focus on meeting stricter academic standards.

- Ninety percent of teachers and 86 percent of parents surveyed connect physical activity with improved academic performance and behavior.

- Ninety-four percent of teachers and 89 percent of parents favor developing new "lifestyle" approaches to physical education, focusing on activities that children can continue to participate in after they've left school.

Adapted, by permission, from the Robert Wood Johnson Foundation's Healthy Schools for Healthy Kids Report.

"Physical education in schools can reach the very students who are most at risk—the overweight child with a bad body image, the uncoordinated student who's never been taught skills, or the shy kid with no confidence—to join a team or engage with others at recess. It is in many ways these kids for whom physical education can do the most good."

Tim McCord,
PE4life Academy director and chair,
Physical Education Department, Titusville
(Pennsylvania) Area School District

Reduces Medical Costs

The cost of overweight and obese citizens to the United States economy is nearly $120 billion annually and growing. Quality, daily physical education can reverse that trend. A worldwide study conducted by the International Council on Sport Science and Physical Education (and financed by the International Olympic Committee) found that $1.00 invested in physical education saves $3.20 in medical costs.

As we examine the state of our nation's health and the rising rate of childhood obesity, it is clear that we should be embracing daily physical activity, not eliminating it. Where else can our children learn about, and participate in, a daily activity that can prolong and enhance their health over a lifetime? What other subject taught in school provides a real solution to a nationwide health crisis?

Thomas Jefferson put it this way: "Exercise and recreation are as necessary as reading. I will say rather more necessary because health is worth more than learning."

"This is not about appearances. The issue here is health. It's about the fact that overweight and obesity increase the risk of cardiovascular diseases, type 2 diabetes, several forms of cancer, breathing problems and other health problems."

David Satcher, MD, PhD,
former U.S. surgeon general

The PE4life Way

PE4life is a nonprofit organization determined to make quality, daily physical education in each of our nation's schools a reality. PE4life sees three key problems with our nation's current physical education system: (1) the dramatic decline in the number of students who are taking physical education on a daily basis; (2) the continued emphasis on the sports model of physical education, which emphasizes team sport skill development and participation at the expense of physical fitness, health and wellness education, and lifelong physical activity skill development and participation; and (3) the assignment of grades to students based on skills and innate abilities rather than effort and progress toward individual goals.

To combat these three key problems, the PE4life Program is about getting kids active now and instilling the lifetime benefits of health and wellness. It's about enabling each student to maintain a physically active lifestyle forever. It means emphasizing fitness and well-being, not athleticism. It eliminates practices that humiliate students. And it assesses students on their progress in reaching personal physical activity and fitness goals. A PE4life Program exposes kids to the fun and long-term benefits of movement; it's that simple. The

"Physical education is the most effective grassroots program available to get children active today and help them establish healthy fitness habits that will last a lifetime."

Jim Baugh, founder, PE4life

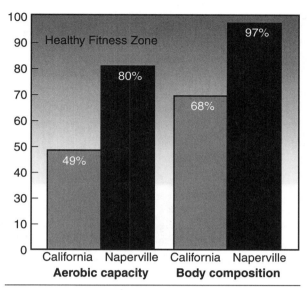

Figure 1 Naperville, Illinois, a PE4life Academy, has a high number of students in the Fitnessgram Healthy Fitness Zone.

PE4life mission statement enforces these ideas: To develop a country of active, healthy children and youth by increasing access to quality physical education solutions. PE4life acts as an advocate, a catalyst for change, and a resource developer to inspire, educate, and empower stakeholders to promote physically active lifestyles for children and youth through quality physical education programs.

Phil Lawler, a veteran physical education teacher and coach, and now a PE4life Academy director, saw the light after a long school day over 15 years ago.

"In the old days, we said, 'Let's run a mile, and if you can't run a mile under 8 minutes, you're a failure.' How many people in this country were turned off to exercise by those standards? I put a heart rate monitor on a young lady, and based on her 13:30 mile, she was a failure. But when I downloaded her heart rate monitor, her average heart rate was 187. By just my observation she wasn't doing anything, but in reality she was working too hard. Now with this technology, we won't make that mistake again. We will personalize it and we'll give kids credit for what they do," said Lawler, who today is director of the Naperville, Illinois, PE4life Academy.

If children take away one thing from their PE4life experience, it should be the importance of daily exercise. Daily physical education is crucial in helping children reap the long-term benefits of physical fitness and establish this healthy habit for life.

PE4life Program Helps Inspire Arkansas Governor to Become PE Advocate

We called Arkansas governor Mike Huckabee and invited him to visit our PE4life Program in Rogers, Arkansas. He accepted and left our program inspired and excited about telling people about the PE program we have and spreading the PE4life message to others. As a result of the visit, the governor featured our PE program on his monthly television program and has used it as a discussion piece during his travels around the country promoting healthy eating and exercise. He happily shares the PE4life philosophy and delivery of the program and instruction he saw in the Rogers public schools.

Governor Huckabee has lost over 100 pounds and has become an avid exerciser.

As the new chairman of the Southern Governor's Council, he will make his health, nutrition, and physical activity platform a priority. Gov. Huckabee has appeared on many local and national radio and television programs touting his passion for physical activity. He regularly mentions the PE4life Program in Rogers. We have received many calls from people who have heard about our program through Gov. Huckabee. We are planning to stay in touch with him and continue to be part of his important message!

Kim Mason,
PE4life Academy director,
Rogers public schools

Making Fitness Count

Melea Smith, APR, director of communications at Naperville, Illinois, CUSD 203 and a member of the Illinois chapter of the National School Public Relations Association, wrote about the importance of activity:

In the midst of national discussion about the alarming rise in childhood obesity, including hot debates over the contents of school vending machines and the quality of school lunches—both important topics—one fact remains: Physical fitness is as much about daily activity levels as it is about caloric intake. To get fit and stay fit, even thin people need exercise.

People in the United States have become fixated on calorie, fat, and carb counts. Yet, experts report that, over the last decade, the average American has increased caloric intake by 1 percent but reduced activity level by 15 percent.

California studies in 2002 linked high academic performance to daily physical activity. While Illinois ranks an abysmal 46th in the nation for educational funding, it is the sole remaining state to require four years of physical education at the secondary level. This just may be a key to success for students seeking higher test scores, as well as for educators working to meet No Child Left Behind mandates.

Promoting an approach known as the new PE, District 203 serves as a laboratory site for PE4life, a Kansas City-based, nonprofit organization promoting daily activity in America's schools. Over the last two years, District 203 has hosted visitors from 26 states, as well as China, Mexico, and Germany. Educators from Australia, Turkey, and Taiwan also have asked for help in rethinking their PE programs. PE4life calculates that the direct impact of these visits exceeds 500,000 students.

"It's phenomenal the things they are doing here," Chris Greathouse said during a recent two-day visit. As the PE department head for Black Forest Academy in Kandern, Germany, Greathouse says that he now has "the vision to take our program to a higher level, for the sake of our kids. I am impressed by the focus on health and wellness I've seen here."

How can a school district with a PE budget of $2 per student per year at the high school level, $1 at the junior high level, and 50 cents at the elementary level achieve this level of success?

"It's a total paradigm shift," says Phil Lawler, a Madison Junior High School physical education teacher, the former PE coordinator of District 203, and cofounder of the program. Lawler now serves as a national spokesperson for PE4life. Gone are dodgeball and the picking of students for teams (with one inevitably being picked last). Treadmills, exercise bikes, and climbing walls that even adaptive PE students learn to traverse replace painful junior high and high school experiences.

"It is a belief system that underpins our curriculum and a tool which supports us, as well as promoting wellness nationwide," explains associate superintendent Lenore Johnson.

The new PE, featured in *Newsweek, Time, USA Today*, and as a centerpiece of a PBS documentary, hasn't attracted national attention by applying for waivers or offering summer school opt-out courses. Instead, it has excelled in the creation of partnerships with parent organizations, the business community, service clubs, and local hospitals to fund the latest in exercise technology.

While many are sacrificing physical education in lieu of increased "core curriculum," the numbers for District 203 indicate that it's not just coincidence that this academically high-performing school district delivers, daily, quality physical education to its 19,000 students.

"What sets us apart is the data we collect, showing that we are, in fact, making a difference," says Paul Zientarski, also a cofounder of the program and PE instructional coordinator at Naperville Central High School. The school tracks fitness levels of students twice each year over their four high school years.

Statistics on district ninth-graders indicated that a remarkable 97.1 percent are in the healthy fitness zone, according to child obesity norms based on body composition testing. Dr. Ken Cooper, founder of the Cooper Institute in Dallas, Texas, and known as the father of aerobics, established these norms. By comparison, California's figures showed that 67 percent of students were in the healthy range.

"Even more startling, in California only 49 percent of kids met the healthy standard for cardiovascular conditioning (based on the mile run), while ours were at 80 percent," notes Zientarski. "The 2002 study correlated that the more fit the kids were, the better they performed academically. It's a part of why our students do as well as they do—it's a total mind, total body educational approach."

Lawler and Zientarski suggest that schools seeking to change their approach to fitness should begin by using their heart monitors.

"Thanks to a partnership with Edward Hospital and its leading cardiologist, Dr. Vincent Bufalino, we were able to begin monitoring students' heart rates. It changed our perception of exercise," Lawler says.

"I found that the kid trailing last in the mile run might actually be working the hardest. This technology also allowed students to become a partner in their own physical fitness."

"You have to empower kids by giving them the freedom to choose, while making them aware of what healthy choices are," Zientarski says. "We're able to maintain our academic integrity and challenge our students in their PE classes by offering a wide variety—from rock climbing to our high-ropes leadership course.

"It's not our job to make students be fit, but rather to provide them with the information and lead them to an awareness of the value and importance of taking care of themselves," Zientarski says. "We don't practice the traditional sports approach, but rather urge individual goal setting. It's more of a fitness club mentality, promoting individualized programs and offering students the chance to take themselves as high as they can.

"We strive for an end result of imparting the intrinsic desire to be fit, along with the knowledge of how to accomplish that—something they can carry with them throughout their lives," Zientarski concludes.

Illinois School Board Journal,
September/October 2004

Secretary of Health Praises PE4life Academy in Titusville, Pennsylvania

"Special things are going on here in Titusville. You are all in a perfect place at which to make a difference. This is not just about physical education or gym class. You are demonstrating about being physically fit. You can't all be star athletes, but you are ahead of the game. You are the fittest kids in the area, maybe in the Commonwealth.

"It was a pleasure to learn more about Titusville's initiative, to meet the people and students who were imperative to its implementation, and to see the surrounding community that has helped make it a success. Witnessing this overall collaboration and commitment demonstrates that Pennsylvania is a leader in preventing and protecting its citizens against public health disparities."

Dr. Calvin Johnson,
Pennsylvania state secretary of health

"I wish physical education was taught across the nation like it is taught in Naperville, Illinois [at the PE4life Academy]. You will end up saving more lives through your profession as a physical education instructor than I will ever be able to as a physician. Please make physical education teachers throughout the country aware of the immense effects their efforts can have in developing a healthier population."

Dr. Michael Kretz,
25-year practicing physician,
Hudson, Wisconsin

Interestingly, people don't think twice about brushing their teeth at least twice a day. We've mastered this daily habit. With our knowledge about the importance of getting the whole body moving, it's amazing that we don't give a higher priority to physical activity on a daily basis.

Just as schools are responsible for teaching our children lifelong skills in mathematics and reading comprehension, they should be responsible for providing students with habits to become active and stay active—for life. Consider this: If children are never introduced to the importance of physical activity in PE class, where and when will they learn it?

The PE4life Way Is Working

The PE4life model is working. The Fitnessgram test, which evaluates students in six fitness-related categories, was used to compare the physical fitness levels of ninth-grade students in Naperville, Illinois (home of the first PE4life Academy) with their ninth-grade, non-PE4life counterparts in California. In all six categories, the Naperville students far outpaced their counterparts in California. In the two most significant categories, aerobic capacity and body composition, the results were significantly in favor of the Naperville kids. For example, of the 1,500 freshmen in Naperville, only 3 percent were found to be overweight or obese.

In contrast, 32 percent of their ninth-grade counterparts in California were overweight or obese.

Parents Vote PE Number-One Curriculum in School

Parents of students at Madison Junior High School, home to the Naperville, Illinois, PE4life Academy, voted physical education the number-one curriculum in the school. An amazing 94.1 percent of Naperville parents were satisfied with the PE curriculum; only 1.8 percent were dissatisfied. Moreover, 68.5 percent were very or completely satisfied with the physical education program. Additionally, Naperville counselors are currently recommending that students take their toughest academic class immediately following physical education whenever possible. Finally, the Centers for Disease Control and Prevention named the Naperville program a model physical education program.

Other PE4life Academies around the country are having similar results. Nevertheless, it must be emphasized that PE4life Academies are premier physical education programs. Achieving results like those that occurred in Naperville won't happen overnight. But every physical education program in the country can start to make small changes toward the lifestyle model of physical education that is the hallmark of every PE4life Academy.

PE4life Academies: Train the Trainers

The PE4life philosophy is to "train the trainers" in the best of what the "new" PE offers. PE4life Academies are exemplary, daily physical education programs. These academies are designed to provide training to other school districts and communities around the country so that they can develop their own PE4life Programs.

The pilot PE4life Academy was established in Naperville (Illinois) School District 203 in October 2001. Today two additional PE4life Academies are operating, one in Grundy Center, Iowa, and another in Titusville, Pennsylvania. Ultimately, PE4life plans to have an academy in every state.

Besides learning about the PE4life Program itself, participants at each PE4life Academy

Students Show Dramatic Improvement

Fourth- and fifth-graders at Woodland Elementary School, in the Kansas City (Missouri) School District, showed dramatic improvement across six health and fitness indicators just one year after starting a PE4life program. In addition, the entire student body at the school showed a dramatic decrease in disciplinary issues (see figure 2).

Prior to being active in a PE4life Program, the students at Woodland Elementary had participated in a 50-minute physical education class only one day per week. However, generous local foundation funding allowed PE4life to help Woodland Elementary establish a PE4life Program. Establishing the program included hiring one additional physical education instructor to offer physical education every day for 45 minutes per day (225 minutes per week), upgraded facilities, new interactive fitness equipment, assessment technology, and the incorporation of the PE4life philosophy into the delivery of PE.

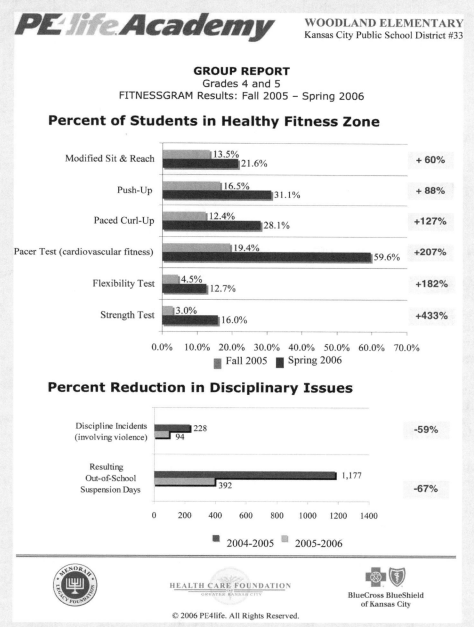

Figure 2 Woodland Elementary School showed drastic improvement across six health and fitness indicators.

receive customized training about how to secure funding from external sources. Moreover, information is provided regarding developing community outreach programs that promote the value of physical education for the community as a whole.

"After visiting their program, I left the PE4life [Academy] with the feeling of a man on a mission. I'm proud to say our program has grown by leaps and bounds using the PE4life [Academy] as a model," said Bryan T. Schwab, health and physical education chairperson at the Oil City (Pennsylvania) Area School District.

PE4life and the PEP Grant

The PE4life initiative started in 1999. The initial focus was to help pass the Physical Education Program (PEP) legislation in the United States Congress. With PE4life playing a prominent role, the PEP legislation passed in 2000. In the years since, over $325 million in PEP grants have helped hundreds of school districts enhance their physical education programs.

The Carol M. White Physical Education Program (PEP) provides grants to local education agencies and community-based organizations. The grants pay 90 percent of the total cost of initiating, expanding, and improving physical education programs.

In January 2004, Congress approved a bill that contained $70 million for PEP grants for 2004. The $70 million translated into approximately 300 grants for school districts across the country to use in improving their physical education programs. This was a major victory for PE4life and other PEP grant advocates. In 2005 the appropriation was $73,408,000, the number of new awards anticipated was 102,

"The bad news is that our nation's childhood obesity epidemic is worsening. The good news is that the most cost-effective delivery system for addressing this epidemic is a quality, daily physical education program that reaches all children."

Anne Flannery, president and CEO, PE4life

"As a professional physical educator, nothing fulfills me more than seeing young students figuring out that one doesn't have to be a sports star to be a healthy, active, self-assured person."

Tim McCord, PE4life Academy director, Titusville, Pennsylvania

and the range of awards was $75,000 to $650,000. To get an application, go to www.ed.gov/programs/whitephysed/applicant.html. You can get updates on the PEP grant by visiting www.pe4life.org.

Additional PE4life Initiatives

PE4life is continually broadening its efforts to bring quality, daily physical education to all K–12 students across the United States. To that end, PE4life is developing several new initiatives, including the following:

- *PE4life Academies.* The academies are exemplary, daily PE programs focused on lifetime, health-related physical activity and fitness. PE4life Academies provide training to school and community leaders with the objective of assisting them with the development of PE4life Programs in their communities.

- *PE4life Programs.* PE4life Programs combine today's best practices in PE to inspire and educate all students about the vital importance of lifetime physical activity and fitness. PE4life Programs incorporate cardiovascular fitness, muscular strength and endurance, and team building and adventure education within the curriculum. The programs use technology and individualized student assessments, and encourage involvement within local health, medical, and business communities.

- *National PE Day®.* PE4life created National PE Day to draw attention to the lifetime health and fitness benefits of quality, daily physical education. Celebrated in early May each year, activities are conducted in Washington, DC, and in communities across the country. Celebrity athletes and physical education advocates gather in Washington for the annual PE4life awards dinner and Congressional PEP rally to deliver the PE4life message to our nation's policymakers. Additionally, schools across the nation host PE4life field days and local advocacy campaigns.

- *PE4life summits.* PE4life annually hosts a number of summits throughout the country on topics such as combating childhood obesity.

These events feature presentations by respected physical education professionals, as well as PE advocates from the education, health care, business, and government sectors. PE4life has now trained people from 48 of the 50 states through its academies and summits. In addition, a number of people from other countries have attended.

How to Use the DVD

The DVD that is packaged with this book provides a comprehensive tool kit of resources that you can use in the development and promotion of a quality PE program. The following is an outline of what is included on the DVD, with brief suggestions on how to use these resources.

PE4life Academy Video
Featuring Phil Lawler

In this video, Phil Lawler (a pioneer in fitness-related programming in public schools) describes how he built his own PE4life Program. This video can be shown in its entirety (click on the Play All button), or you can go to a specific step because Phil's clips have been divided into segments that match the steps a school can take to develop their program, which are covered in the first seven chapters of the book. At the beginning of the menu, there is a brief video introduction by Phil Lawler. This introduction is the ideal starting point when using this DVD for an in-service, workshop, or similar presentation.

Please note that many of the examples support a number of topics. For example, the fitness equipment footage in the "Get Equipped" step also provides excellent ideas for the "Pinpoint Funding Opportunities" step. The "Community Support/Climbing Wall" footage also works for the "Pinpoint Funding Opportunities" step since it explains a "value-in-kind" donation of the artist's time. This video makes an excellent visual for any in-service or workshop. You can show the entire video and then discuss how it applies to your school, or you can show one step at a time, discuss it, and then move on to the next step. It is also an excellent tool to use in a college PE methods course to initiate student discussion. In addition, you could use it as part of a presentation to a school board, curriculum committee, or PTA if your audience is interested in learning details of a quality program. If the time you have to make an impact with an audience is short, the video described next is the one to use.

PE4life Community Action Video

This 10-minute video, created to show to various groups in support of quality PE, is designed to catch the attention of key decision makers in a short period of time. It serves as the ideal starting point of any presentation you might make to a PTA, school board, legislator, and other stakeholder, while also being a great video to show PE majors in a methods course to help get them thinking about how to advocate for their future profession.

Reading, 'Riting, 'Rithmetic, and Running: Exercise and the Brain

This video excerpt is taken from a presentation by Dr. John Ratey, assistant clinical professor of psychiatry at Harvard University Medical School. Dr. Ratey made this presentation on his research into the positive impact of exercise on brain function and learning to the DuPage County, Illinois, Regional Office of Education physical education in-service in early 2006. This video is an excellent choice to show at a community presentation on the value of supporting PE, to show to teachers at a workshop or in-service, or to show PE majors.

DVD-ROM Content

The material contained in the DVD-ROM section of this DVD can only be accessed using a DVD-ROM drive in a computer (not a DVD player on a television). To access the folders (PE4life Community Action Kit, Blueprint for Change, Reproducible Forms, or PE Resource Web Sites), follow these instructions:

1. Place DVD in the DVD-ROM drive of your computer.
2. Open "My Computer" and right click on the DVD-ROM drive.
3. Select "Open."
4. Double click the "Contents" folder.
5. Double click the folder that contains the information you want and make the appropriate selection.

The following is information about the content in the individual folders on the DVD-ROM.

- PE4life Academy Presentation. This PowerPoint presentation covers the PE4life way, including the seven steps to developing a quality program. It is the ideal companion to this book and can be used as the basis for an in-service using this book as the manual. It is also an excellent lecture tool for professors who have adopted this book for a PE course.

- PE4life Community Action Kit. In this kit you'll find ready-to-use PowerPoint presentations, handouts, and sample letters to use in advocating for quality PE. If you are planning a presentation to a school board, PTA, legislators, or community group, these resources are designed to help.

- Blueprint for Change Document. The Blueprint for Change is a 10 step action plan to help children become healthier through quality, daily PE programs and increased physical activity. The Blueprint was produced by PE4life. This document provides an excellent starting point for any individual or group interested in improving the quality of their PE program.

- Reproducible Forms. Here you will find reproducible forms from the book that you can print out and use.

- PE Resource Web Sites. In this section, you will find a document with an extensive list of Web addresses that provide information relating to national PE standards, resources, programs, companies, and so on. This list provides an easy way to copy and paste the Web addresses from the document to a computer's Internet browser.

The main screen from the PE4life DVD-ROM.

BUILDING A PE4life ACTION PLAN

CHAPTER 1

Build Your Community-Based PE Team

Organizing Your Team

The first step in developing your PE4life Program is building a support system for your cause. Recruiting other champions of quality, daily physical education broadens the support to include others who see the need for children to develop physically. Your recruitment gives them a role.

Begin by thinking about who might share your vision and by creating a team to support it. For a PE4life Program to become a reality in your school, school district, or community, a community-wide team effort is essential. The first job is to build a PE advisory group made up of physical education advocates from a variety of areas in your community.

Next, identify and organize a group of people, such as teachers, administrators, school board members, parents, members of the medical community, civic and business leaders, and other allies, to discuss your ideas for change within the school and school district's PE program. Think broadly, never limiting the possibilities. In most cases, the physical education teacher with the PE4life vision will serve as the leader for the group. Moving forward, this group will set the foundation for all future improvements. Here are some examples of potential allies who will likely have the vision and support your mission:

Other physical educators—Enlist the help of fellow physical education instructors within your school, school district, and surrounding school districts or across the country. Also, consider college and university physical education professors in your region.

The Internet can help you keep in touch with other physical educators who support your goals. For example, stay in touch with

fellow PE4life Academy graduates through cyberspace. Also, on the PE4life Web site, www. pe4life.org, you can chat online and exchange ideas with physical education advocates across the country. For another excellent resource, check out the National Association for Sport and Physical Education (NASPE) PE Talk electronic mailing list at the www.sportime.com Web site. Fellow members of NASPE or the American Alliance for Health, Physical Education, Recreation and Dance (AAHPERD) are also good potential sources of support.

Administrators—Administrators are looking for demonstrable results. Accountability is a survival issue for physical education. A PE4life Program can help immensely in this area because it can provide administrators and board members with data from tests that objectively measure student improvement on health and wellness measures. When you effectively demonstrate to administrators the benefits of a quality physical education program, including evidence of improved academic performance, recruiting them as PE advocates becomes much easier. By showing how your vision

will contribute to the overall school mission, you've begun to pave the way for implementation of your program. Remember that two key stakeholder groups are on your side: A recent study revealed that 81 percent of teachers and 85 percent of parents favor requiring students to take physical education every day at every grade level.

Parents—What is more fundamental than good health? Virtually all parents want to ensure the health and wellness of their children. By clearly articulating your vision of quality physical education, and demonstrating its short- and long-term benefits, you effectively become an advocate of children's health in parents' eyes. Parents who understand your goals will welcome you onto their team and join you on yours.

Health care providers—Many schools and school districts that have made the paradigm shift to a health and wellness focus in physical education have done so with the strong support of local hospitals, doctors, public health nurses, and other professionals in the medical community. Finding partners in the medical field in your community should be a top priority (see "Me and Dr. Bufalino" on page 6).

Community organizations—Rotary Clubs, Kiwanis, and other community organizations are always looking for good causes to support. Increasing the well-being of children in the community is often a top priority of these groups.

Businesses—Most businesses seek good opportunities for community relations. Media coverage of the childhood obesity problem in this country and the related medical problems has been extensive recently. Moreover, companies are increasingly aware of the economic costs

> "The unique thing about schools, we have every employee of every company in the United States in our schools today . . . companies cannot afford to hire this next generation . . . because of health care alone. [Companies] need to work together with us to solve this problem."
>
> *Phil Lawler,*
> *PE4life Academy director,*
> *Naperville, Illinois*

Five Hours of PE a Week Could Cut Obesity and Overweight by 43 Percent

A Rand Corporation study based on long-term U.S. Department of Education data found that the prevalence of obesity and overweight among girls fell 10 percent in schools that gave first-graders one hour more of exercise time per week than they gave to kindergartners. Drawing on that finding, the researchers believe that giving kindergartners at least five hours of physical education time per week—the amount recommended by the federal government—could potentially reduce the prevalence of obesity and overweight among girls by 43 percent.

"This has the ability to affect tens of thousands, if not hundreds of thousands, of children. The implications are so big because this is something we can do as a society," said Nancy Chockley, president of the National Institute for Health Care Management Foundation, a Washington, DC-based non-profit group that released a research brief on the study.

In the past decade, many schools have scaled back recess time or physical education classes to provide more time to prepare students for testing programs that are a key part of school-funding formulas, according to Dr. Vincent Ferrandino, executive director of the National Association of Elementary School Principals.

"Many of those schools that made those choices to cut back on PE classes now realize that was not a good decision in regard to their students' health," said Ferrandino.

of physical inactivity. Make your case to them and watch how quickly support can follow. For example, in West Virginia an insurance company donated $500,000 to put a new piece of fitness equipment in all high schools statewide. Consider which businesses in your area to approach. The local chamber of commerce is often an excellent place to start.

Civic leaders—Political figures can be powerful allies in the fight for quality, daily physical education programs in your community. The physical inactivity epidemic affecting our youth (and the resulting health ramifications) is a hot issue for many civic leaders. You can leverage their influence to great advantage.

Developing Goals and Setting Priorities

Your PE advisory group can begin with the following activities:

• Start exploring best practices. You'll find many examples of successful and innovative PE4life activities in this manual. You'll also see examples and hear about others during your PE4life Academy training. In addition, the PE4life Academy is a great opportunity to tap into the minds of your peers. Identify a model for your future program and begin laying the groundwork for achieving that vision.

• As a group, conduct a situation analysis of your school's current physical education program (strengths, weaknesses, opportunities, threats, and so on). Develop a vision for your program.

• Develop short- and long-term goals for your physical education department. Make sure that everyone in the department, as well as other key stakeholders (e.g., administrators, community stakeholders), is involved. Discuss goals for early childhood, elementary, middle school, and high school. Start with the result in mind. What do you want your students to know and be able to do physically by the time that they "graduate" from physical education?

Me and Dr. Bufalino

The first thing I did when seeking support for our physical education program was to align with a local doctor. I have always felt physical education teachers are the Rodney Dangerfields of education . . . "absolutely no respect." So, I figured I needed the voice of a medical doctor to help convince the community of the value of a quality physical education program.

Fortunately, our community was home to Dr. Vincent Bufalino, a very high-profile cardiologist who had a strong interest in children. Dr. Bufalino was one of the first doctors in the country to study the cholesterol levels of children ages 10 to 17. He was dismayed to find more than 40 percent of the children in his study had elevated cholesterol. Dr. Bufalino said he was much more interested in preventing heart disease than treating it. As such, he was excited about forming a partnership with our physical education program. As the partnership progressed, we teamed with Dr. Bufalino and the local hospital in offering cholesterol screenings during physical education class in all of our junior and senior high schools. This volunteer program has been a huge success.

Our partnership with the local media community has continued to evolve. One of our most successful medical initiatives has been the creation of our school district medical advisory board. This committee has developed into a great tool for improving communication and improving children's health in our community. Early, we had a difficult time convincing medical people with busy schedules to commit to serving on this committee. The first year there were only a few doctors interested. Seven years later, we had more than 40 doctors meeting for over two hours. Besides doctors, a committee of this nature can include school nurses, athletics trainers, social workers, school administrators, and physical education teachers.

Several very successful programs have developed in our district as a result of this partnership with the medical field. One is our asthma policy. In today's world, all physical education teachers are being forced to deal with an ever-increasing number of students with asthma. Our community put together a committee made up of asthma specialists, parents, nurses, and physical education teachers and developed district guidelines for dealing with asthma. Doctors are now aware that we modify our programs for kids with asthma and other medical conditions and illnesses. As a result, in our high schools, we have almost eliminated medical excuses for PE. Our community doctors now know that our physical education programs are more than just glorified recess and, in fact, are a true prescription for improving children's health.

A medical advisory board is something every school district in the nation should adopt. Such a program can be put in place immediately with no expenses.

Phil Lawler,
PE4life Academy director,
Naperville, Illinois

• Prioritize the changes that you would like to make in your PE program—successful implementation will depend on a variety of factors, including the resources available (personnel, finances, time, and so on). For example, should you first implement technology tools (heart rate monitors, fitness assessment software such as Tri-Fit or Fitnessgram/Activitygram, and the like), construct a wellness center, or update your curriculum? The order of tackling changes depends on you and the opportunities you see.

While developing your goals and organizing your program, realize that in the first year you need not accomplish all the steps being shared here. Building a quality physical education program is a long-term investment. Small steps are appropriate. You will face obstacles (which we discuss in chapter 7), and thus the more help that you can get from significant members of your community, the better.

Extending Activity Outside the School

Judith Rink, a professor at the University of South Carolina, offers these suggestions:

1. Create opportunities within the school for students to be active outside of the required gym period. Add fitness and sports programs before school, after school, and during recess.

2. Make physical education teachers "directors of physical activity" whose job it is to coordinate efforts within the school to increase participation in physical activity among students, teachers, and staff.

3. Collaborate with the community. Use the services of local recreation centers, tennis courts, swimming pools, and fitness clubs, and invite fitness and health professionals to share their expertise with the students.

4. Reward participation in physical activity outside of the school milieu. High schools in North Carolina require students to participate in some form of community-based physical activity like fitness or dance classes at the local YMCA or to join a local sports league. The program is designed to encourage students to take responsibility for their own fitness.

Reprinted by permission of Dr. Judith Rink.

Identify physical education stakeholders that could be potential members of your PE advisory group.

Other physical educators

_____

_____

Administrators

_____

_____

Parents

_____

_____

Health care providers

_____

_____

Community organizations

_____

_____

Businesses (e.g., CEOs of corporations)

_____

_____

Civic leaders

_____

_____

Consider the current situation with your physical education program.

Strengths

_____

_____

Weaknesses

_____

_____

Opportunities

_____

_____

Threats

_____

_____

Develop a vision of your ideal physical education program.

_____

_____

How can you and your team make the transition from a school-based physical education program to a community-based physical education program?

_____

_____

List key factors and issues affecting your current situation.

_____

_____

List your short-term goals.

_____

_____

List your long-term goals.

_____

_____

Take the Next Steps

What are your priorities for the following time frames?

Next six months

First year

_____   _____

_____   _____

_____   _____

Step 1: Implementation Plan

Task	Who is responsible?	When will it be completed?

Document the Results

What results did you see at the following times?

Six months

_____

_____

One year

Two years

_____   _____

_____   _____

_____   _____

From *PE4life: Developing and Promoting Quality Physical Education,* by PE4life, 2007, Champaign, IL: Human Kinetics.

CHAPTER 2

Develop an Advocacy Strategy

Promoting the PE4life Way

Making your PE4life Program a success will take hard work. For one thing, you will have to become a champion of quality, daily PE in schools—a change agent, so to speak. One of the goals of PE4life is to help you become an effective change agent.

Being an effective change agent means believing in your mission, rounding up allies to support your cause, developing creative new partnerships, and effectively communicating why PE4life is crucial to the health and wellness of our children. Keep in mind that being an effective advocate for your program requires constant effort. Every year, you'll face a new group of parents, teachers, and administrators whom you will have to educate about the benefits of quality, daily physical education.

In this section, we'll explore steps that you can take to jump-start your advocacy efforts. But remember, the most important step is to be your own best advocate, to believe in your program and the value that it provides. Then persuade others—parents, colleagues, doctors, local businesses, civic leaders—to join your cause.

"We must have a passion for teaching—I tell everyone that I teach the most important subject in school. I truly believe physical education is the most important subject taught in school. I trust that all teachers think that way about their subjects. Six years ago I was training for a half-marathon and in the best shape of my life when I was diagnosed with cancer. Living my subject matter on a daily basis literally saved my life. I don't know how many teachers of other subjects can say that."

Rick Schupbach,
PE4life Academy director,
Grundy Center, Iowa

Launching Your Advocacy Efforts

The key to launching your advocacy efforts is to get your ducks in a row first. The following steps will help you do this.

Gather Your Resources

You already know the importance of quality, daily physical education. But to convey the benefits to others, you'll need to start gathering information and resources to support your message. Fortunately, countless facts support the need for increased physical activity among children. Some of them are detailed in this manual (see the introduction). You can also visit www.pe4life.org and NASPE at www.aahperd.org/naspe, both of which feature many links to research information, current news articles, and other important resources on this issue. In particular, you can use our "Blueprint for Change" (on the enclosed DVD), developed by PE4life's Center for the Advancement of Physical Education (CAPE), at www.pe4life.org. Also, you can use the PE4life Community Action Kit resources that we have placed on the enclosed DVD to help you launch your advocacy efforts.

Create a Mission Statement That You Can Share

Now that you're armed with the facts, you and your team will need to craft key messages that will resonate with parents, administrators, other teachers, and the community at large. Creating a simple mission statement will help you sell your program. An effective mission statement must convey the primary objective of your program (see chapter 9 for more details).

In selling your PE4life Program, you need to consider the benefits that your program can provide to all students, the benefits that only physical education can provide, and the benefits that all parents, administrators, community members, and other teachers can support. Not all parents, for example, care whether their children learn how to play baseball or basketball. But all parents care about the short- and long-term health of their children. Benefits available to all children make physical education important to everyone.

Remember, attending PE4life Academy is the first step toward developing a PE4life Program, and the name PE4life conveys the idea that the health and wellness benefits that you are providing are for life.

The medical costs related to sedentary lifestyles and poor nutrition are skyrocketing. So is the number of preventable deaths that occur each year. Quality, daily physical education is the best method that we have to prepare children to be physically active, healthy, and productive adults. We need to share this message continually.

Build Partnerships to Support Your Team

Besides recruiting good people for your PE advisory group, you'll also want to build alliances with other organizations and businesses that share your mission of helping children learn how to live healthy, physically active lives. For example, seriously consider connecting with people in the medical community. Invite them to your PE4life Program and let them watch and learn how you teach the importance of daily physical activity to your students. Here are some external allies that may share your team's mission:

- Fire and police departments
- Hospitals and medical clinics
- Your state chapter of the American Alliance for Health, Physical Education, Recreation and Dance (AAHPERD)
- Fitness centers
- Parks and recreation departments
- YMCAs and Boys and Girls Clubs
- Youth sport leagues
- Insurance companies and HMOs
- Running clubs
- Dance, gymnastics, and martial arts studios
- Private athletic and health clubs
- PTAs

Visit these organizations and discuss how you could work together to promote physical activity in your community. In particular, building a strong alliance with a local hospital can be extremely beneficial in gaining credibility for

Example: Naperville, Illinois, School District 203

District 203 PE4life Program Mission Statement

The Physical Education Department, as well as Naperville School District 203, has made a commitment to prepare students to live healthy, productive, and physically active lives for the 21st century.

- Our PE4life Program will provide all students with a variety of challenges that will contribute to the development and maintenance of their physical, cognitive, and affective well-being.
- Students will be provided with the foundation for making informed decisions that will empower them to achieve and maintain a healthy lifestyle.

- Physical education is a lifelong process, one that is the primary responsibility of the student, shared by home, district, and community.

District 203 Physical Education Curriculum Belief Statements

- The following strands must be interwoven into the K–12 physical education curriculum: movement skills; fitness education; team building; cognitive skills, literacy, and technology.
- Quality, daily physical education is essential, K–12.
- Delivery of quality instruction requires certified physical educators.

---

your program. Moreover, your community hospital is likely to have an experienced director of marketing and public relations who could help you gain media and community exposure for your program. Remember that the hospital also wants to see its community physically active and healthy.

Delivering Your Message to All the Right Audiences

Now that you've built your team, completed your mission statement, and begun to develop partnerships in the community, you are ready to put together an advocacy plan for each of your target audiences. The objective of the plan is to find the best way to work together to develop a PE4life Program.

When you believe in your mission and are armed with the right resources, pitching your case to external audiences will come naturally. You can do it! Be the change!

Here are some key target audiences, as well as examples of creative ways in which you can reach out to them:

- *Parents.* The parents in your community will be a key group for you to cultivate. But keep in mind that their only experience with PE may have been a negative one. Take time to reeducate them about the importance of quality, daily PE. Demonstrate how you are changing your PE program to benefit all students. Let them know that quality PE focuses more on effort than it does on comparing students to each other. Explain why their child's well-being is your top priority (see figure 2.1). Parents won't ignore the startling nationwide statistics on childhood obesity and inactivity when you personalize the issue to their own child's long-term health and wellness! Consider the following tactics to get parents on board:

- Build a Web site for the program that parents can access to get updates and information about students, their activities and progress, and upcoming activities.
- Send home a newsletter that describes your program. Include health and wellness tips for parents and offer them creative ideas for being active with their

children. You can find a newsletter template at www.pe4life.org.

- Hold a physical education open house at school. Students can demonstrate some of the innovative things that you're doing in class, and you can offer a Q&A session to provide additional information to parents.
- Ask to speak to the PTA about quality, daily physical education. The PE4life Community Action Kit (found on the DVD) provides a video and handouts that you can use.
- Celebrate National PE Day® in the first week in May each year and invite parents and community leaders to take part in the activities. Check out www.pe4life.org for information and resources on celebrating National PE Day®.

- *Administrators and teachers.* You'll constantly have to play the role of PE advocate with your administrators and fellow teachers. These groups can provide tremendous support and resources in ways that you may not have envisioned. For example, your school's technology director may become a strong advocate for quality, daily PE and help you locate funding for new technology equipment for your PE program. A few ideas to advocate PE to your coworkers could include the following:

- Ask to give an in-service for the teachers, administrators, and other staff in your building on a topic like weight control, heart health, or stress reduction through physical activity.
- Present cross-curriculum learning ideas in a staff meeting. For example, reinforce math skills by having students

estimate how many times a healthy heart beats in one year.

- Distribute informational resources to staff members on the health and wellness challenges that our children face and the role of physical education in addressing them. Visit www.pe4life.org for resources, including our "Blueprint for Change" (found on the DVD) and current articles.
- Post informational posters that describe quality physical education and its benefits in the gym or hallways.
- Organize a schoolwide PE activity, such as a walk-a-thon.
- Invite teachers and administrators to support and join National PE Day activities.

"In order to reach out to the parents of my elementary students, I host a PE night at the PTA at least once a year. Last year, I used a video camera throughout the year to record the variety of activities in which the students had participated. For the PTA presentation, I produced a 15-minute video with shots of the parents' children participating in a wide variety of activities—it was a big hit. It was a great way to educate parents about the important things their children were learning in PE. In addition, I used the PE4life Community Action Kit, which helped me convey the value of my program to the health and wellness of the students."

KaCee Chambers,
elementary PE teacher,
Olathe, Kansas

"We need to convince parents and school boards that PE has evolved. It can be a valuable part of a child's development. With rising rates of obesity, it can also save their lives."

Judy Young,
vice president of programs for
AAHPERD

FITNESSGRAM®

Report for Parents

Charlie Brown
Grade: 7   Age: 13
Jefferson Middle School

People come in all shapes and sizes, but everyone can benefit from regular physical activity and a healthy level of physical fitness. The FITNESSGRAM fitness test battery evaluates five different parts of health-related fitness, including aerobic capacity, muscular strength, muscular endurance, flexibility, and body composition. Parents play an important role in shaping children's physical activity and dietary habits. This report will help you evaluate your child's current level of health-related fitness and help you identify ways to promote healthy lifestyles in your family.

Instructor: Kathy Read

	Date	Height	Weight
Current:	09/20/2006	5' 5"	137 lbs

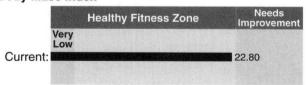

	Needs Improvement	Healthy Fitness Zone

The PACER
Current: ▇▇▇▇ 44

VO2max is based on your aerobic test score. It shows your ability to do activities such as running, cycling, or sports at a high level. HFZ begins at 42.

VO2Max
Current: 46

(Abdominal) Curl-Up
Current: ▇▇▇▇▇ 24

(Trunk Extension) Trunk Lift
Current: ▇▇▇▇▇ 10

(Upper Body) Push-Up
Current: ▇▇▇▇ 15

(Flexibility) Shoulder Stretch R, L
Current: ▇▇▇▇▇▇▇▇ Y, Y

AEROBIC CAPACITY

Aerobic capacity is a measure of the ability of the heart, lungs, and muscles to perform sustained physical activity. In general, the more your child exercises, the higher his or her aerobic capacity level will be. Aerobic capacity is measured with the PACER test, the one-mile run, or the walk test.
Importance: Good aerobic capacity can reduce risks of heart disease, stroke, and diabetes. Although generally not present in children, these diseases can begin during childhood and adolescence.

Healthy Fitness Zone for 13 year-old boys = 41 - 83 laps

MUSCLE STRENGTH, ENDURANCE, & FLEXIBILITY

These components of health-related fitness measure the overall fitness of the musculoskeletal system. A variety of tests are used to assess these different components.
Importance: The fitness level of muscles is important for injury prevention and overall body function. Strength, endurance, and flexibility are important for maintaining good posture, low back health, and total body function.

Healthy Fitness Zone for 13 year-old boys
Curl-Up = 21 - 40 repetitions
Trunk Lift = 9 - 12 inches
Push-Up = 12 - 25 repetitions
Shoulder Stretch = Must be Yes on R & L

BODY COMPOSITION

The body composition measure refers to the relative proportion of fat and lean tissue in the body. Body fat percentage can be estimated by skinfold calipers or other measuring devices. The Body mass index (BMI) is another indicator that determines if a person is at a healthy weight for his or her height.
Importance: Overweight youth are at high risk for being overweight adults. Adult obesity is associated with a number of chronic health problems. Many of these health problems can begin early in life. It is important to begin healthy eating and regular activity early.

Healthy Fitness Zone for 13 year-old boys = 15.10 - 23.00

Body Mass Index

Healthy Fitness Zone	Needs Improvement
Very Low	

Current: ▇▇▇▇▇▇▇▇ 22.80

Being too lean or too heavy may be a sign of (or lead to) health problems. However, not all people who are outside the Healthy Fitness Zone are at risk for health problems. For example, a person with a lot of muscle may have a high BMI without excess fat.

INTERPRETING THE FITNESSGRAM REPORT

Health-related fitness includes a variety of factors. With regular physical activity most children will be able to score in the Healthy Fitness Zone for most of the tests. It is important for all children to be physically active every day (a total of 60 minutes is recommended) even if they are already fit. If your child is in the Needs Improvement area on a particular test, it is important to provide additional opportunities to be active so they can improve their levels of fitness.

Please refer to the back page of the parent report for a description of the Healthy Fitness Zone and for tips on promoting physical activity in your family.

Figure 2.1 The Fitnessgram's parent report is an excellent vehicle for communicating with parents, which is crucial to gaining support for your program.

Physical Activity Enhances Brain Function

The fact that physical activity enhances brain function is important information to use in your advocacy efforts. Here is the basic information that you can share.

Movement accelerates the flow of key nutrients to the brain, like oxygen and glucose. Shortage of oxygen in the brain results in disorientation, confusion, fatigue, sluggishness, and concentration and memory problems. Vigorous activity in a physical education class provides needed nutrients to the brain.

A variety of brain research findings support the importance of quality, daily physical education:

- Swedish neuroscientist Dr. Germund Hesslow says that all things being equal, a physically active child will have an advantage in learning and an inactive child will be at a disadvantage for learning.
- Mental focus and concentration levels in young children improve significantly after they engage in structured physical activity.
- Vigorous aerobic exercise improves short-term memory, creativity, and reaction time.
- Numerous studies have found that students who are involved in athletics generally have higher grades and standardized test scores than their peers who are not involved in athletics.
- Children who engage in daily physical education show superior motor fitness, academic performance, and attitude toward school as compared with their counterparts who do not have physical education.
- Dr. John Ratey of Harvard Medical School found that regular exercise has the same effect as antidepressant drugs because of the positive effect of exercise on mood-altering neurotransmitters in the brain. He points out that cancer patients experienced a 40 percent drop in depression while on a regular exercise program. (See Dr. Ratey on the enclosed DVD.)
- According to neurokinesiologist Jean Blaydes-Madigan, "Movement, physical activity, and exercise change the learning state into one appropriate for retention and retrieval of memory, the effects lasting as much as 30 to 60 minutes depending on the student. This evidence is a sound argument for daily, quality physical education and/ or recess."

"Twelve minutes of exercise at 85 percent of your maximum heart rate is like taking a little bit of Prozac and a little bit of Ritalin in a very holistic manner."

John Ratey, MD,
professor of psychiatry,
Harvard Medical School

Getting Help From the Community

Other organizations and businesses share your mission of helping children learn how to live healthy, physically active lives. You should seek to develop partnerships with organizations in your community to build your PE program.

The medical community in Owensboro, Kentucky, determined that engaging the community's youth in a program to change lifestyles through physical fitness and awareness was the best way to establish a healthier community.

In 2000 a children's health assessment showed a significant increase in the number of overweight children and the incidence of diabetes, which drew concern from Owensboro Mercy Health System, the three area school districts, and corporate leaders within the community. Together, they decided that an important step in maintaining health and developing awareness about physical activity was to have a school nurse present in each school and to require in-school health education classes at least once a month for each student.

Medical Community

Tap into the medical community for powerful support. You'll find that health professionals will be one of your best allies in advancing your program, and they lend immediate credibility to your cause. A relationship with a hospital, an individual doctor, or a medical organization can open many doors for your program.

• Encourage your school district to host a group of doctors, nurses, and other members of the medical community for an in-depth discussion about how to improve the health and wellness of children in your schools. This type of mutual discussion can go a long way toward eliminating unnecessary medical excuses for physical education classes and can lead to joint policies such as asthma management guidelines (see "Me and Dr. Bufalino" on page 6).

As a health care delivery system, we've believed for a long time that no matter how much money we throw at the disease/treatment side of medicine, we will never be able to improve the health of our communities the way a quality physical education program for children will."

*Greg Carlson, former CEO,
Owensboro Mercy Medical Park,
Owensboro, Kentucky*

"One of the most significant concerns from a public health perspective is that we know a lot of children who are overweight grow up to be overweight and obese adults, and thus at greater risk for some major health problems such as heart disease and diabetes. One critical answer to this problem is that we all must work together to help our children make physical activity a lifelong habit."

*Dr. Julie Gerberding, director,
Centers for Disease
Control and Prevention*

• Team up with a hospital or clinic to conduct cholesterol or diabetes screenings during physical education classes. Medical professionals are increasingly using two relatively new indicators for early detection—the HbA1C for diabetes and the C-reactive protein for assessing risk of cardiovascular disease.

While researching viable solutions to improve physical fitness in the schools and to increase the future health of the area's students, the group from Owensboro discovered the PE4life Academy in Naperville, Illinois. A community coalition consisting of employees from the Owensboro Mercy Health Park and faculty from area schools made the trip to Naperville and were impressed by Naperville's state-of-the-art approach to physical education and its modern facility. Excited by what they saw, the Owensboro contingent returned to Kentucky and began to work on a similar program of their own.

Funding provided through a partnership between the Mercy Health System, several local corporations, and the area school districts enabled the town of 90,000 to purchase the equipment necessary to establish a state-of the-art physical education program in the six middle schools and two high schools. The cost of restructuring the physical education program was $50,000 to $75,000 per school. All six middle schools and two high schools have new PE4life Programs up and running.

Partnering for Cholesterol Screenings

In Naperville the PE4life Program has developed a partnership with the medical community to educate students and parents. The local hospital offers cholesterol screenings in the school, opening up doors of communication with parents. The statistics on obesity and diabetes become more personal and important for parents when their children are the focus. For example, after a cholesterol screening, the president of the school PTA, whose 13-year-old son was a slender, three-sport athlete, asked me about her son's screening. When she learned that her son's cholesterol count was 240, she commented that her "dining room is her van" and that she needed to make some changes. The screening positively affected the health of an entire family.

In another case, a 12-year-old girl had just gotten her postcard with her cholesterol score. She commented that she got a 200 and was very happy. Because 200 is high, I talked to the student, who then told me that last year her count was 230 and that her entire family had started looking at what they could do to make some improvements.

Does having cholesterol screenings in your school sound expensive? The hospital charges a minimal fee for screening. Some students can't afford the cost of the screening, so other funds are found to pay for them (e.g., the PTA). In addition, if a student gets a really good score, there is no reason to take the test yearly. Beyond the school walls, if one of our kids goes in for a physical today, he or she is more likely to be tested for cholesterol in the future because the in-school training has raised parent awareness.

Phil Lawler,
PE4life Academy director,
Naperville, Illinois

Extended Community

An ongoing goal should be to extend PE beyond the walls of the gymnasium by reaching out to community partners who will provide resources and offer role models. Think broadly in terms of the types of people, businesses, and organizations that may provide support. You'll be surprised at how energized and committed they become as they begin to realize the positive effect that your movement will have on the community at large.

• Show them! The most powerful way to effect change is not just to educate people about what's happening in PE but to have them actually become involved in PE. Invite parents, seniors, and students to come in and work out. Demonstrate how heart rate monitors work. Offer fitness assessments, cholesterol screenings, and blood screenings to community members. Let them see that a PE4life Program is a big leap from the gym class that they might remember.

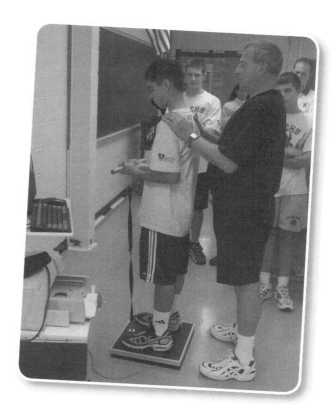

- Ask to speak at a school board meeting regarding the importance of quality, daily physical education. Again, the PE4life Community Action Kit provides video and handouts that you can use. PE4life's "Blueprint for Change" is perfect for this audience.

- Ask the local shopping mall director if your students can present a lesson on lifetime fitness at the mall on a Saturday. You might include a demonstration of heart rate monitors and pedometers. You could also hand out information on the importance of active lifestyles.

- Reach out to your local retirement home. Elementary students in Naperville, Illinois, play games with the residents of the local retirement home as part of a junior and senior Olympics. The retirees share stories about why physical activity is important, and everyone participates in the various games together. What better way to demonstrate the power of PE for life!

"Our goal is to extend PE beyond the walls of the gymnasium and into our community. The most powerful way to do this is not only to educate people about what we're doing in PE but to have them get involved in PE. Our fitness center, located in our junior/senior high school, is truly a community resource. We have junior and senior high students working out side by side with adults and senior citizens. What a powerful message we send to our students when we as adults model for them what to do instead of telling them what to do."

Rick Schupbach,
PE4life Academy director,
Grundy Center, Iowa

- Team up with the local fire or police department on a program that highlights the importance of physical fitness. Hold the event at a community recreation center or other public venue.

Media

Don't underestimate the power of publicity. For PE4life schools across the country, strong public relations plans have proven to be one of the most effective ways to galvanize community support. The physical inactivity epidemic that is affecting our young people, and its negative health ramifications, including obesity, diabetes, high blood pressure, and depression, is a hot issue with the media today. The time is right to reach out to the media with a sound public relations strategy.

- Learn the names of the education editors at your local newspapers and find out who covers schools for your local TV stations. Cultivate a relationship with those reporters so that when something

Turning to Local Heroes for Inspiration

In an effort to reach out to our community, I invited local firefighters to exercise with my middle school students in their PE classes. Because of the outstanding facilities and the opportunity to exercise side by side with impressionable adolescents, the firefighters were eager to work out with the PE classes. It provided a tremendous source of motivation for the PE students to watch these tremendous role models in action. Not only do they watch these heroes exercise to keep their bodies fit, but they take note when the pagers go off and the firefighters rush out the door to perform their duties. In return for the invitation from our PE4life Program, the firefighters now provide first-aid classes to our middle school students.

Phil Lawler,
PE4life Academy director,
Naperville, Illinois

newsworthy happens, they already know who you are and will be more likely to cover your story.

• Regularly feed your media contacts the latest studies and research findings surrounding the physical inactivity epidemic. Add a personal note about what the findings mean for your local school and community and any measures that you've taken, or are planning to take, to address the challenges.

• When something newsworthy happens, let the media know! Enlist the help of your school or school district's communications or PR director to create a press release, and develop compelling messages that will resonate with the news media. Use every opportunity with the media to explain why you're doing what you're doing—how the students (and community) will benefit in both the short and long run. Don't become a pest to reporters, but do let them know when you have a good story to tell.

For example, if your local Rotary group volunteers to buy an obstacle course for your school so that children can learn about heart health, notify newspaper and television reporters. Invite them to observe the students' first use of the obstacle course. (Remember to invite representatives of the Rotary club as well.) Likewise, invite reporters to visit a class where students are using heart rate monitors. Encourage the reporter to put on a monitor. TV reporters are always looking for stories that have compelling visual images.

• Hold a National PE Day® event at your school. Offer media-friendly demonstrations of new equipment, lifetime health and wellness activities, testing, small-sided sports that get all students involved and active (e.g., 3v3 soccer), and the like.

Reaching Out to the Media

Don't be afraid to bring in the media. Share what you're doing, what you've learned, and where you'd like to go in the future. The power of the media has played a crucial part in the development of our program. We have been featured in numerous local newspaper articles, as well as on all of the area television affiliates. On a national level, our program has been featured in the *American School Board Journal* and mentioned in articles appearing in *Time, Newsweek,* and *U.S. News and World Report.* The media coverage has also led to the discovery of our program by numerous schools throughout the state and region. More than 50 school districts have visited Titusville in the last couple of years, "borrowing" ideas from our PE4life Program to assist in the improvement of their own physical education programs. Our proactive approach with the media is a big reason why.

Tim McCord,
PE4life Academy director,
Titusville, Pennsylvania

• Provide reporters with other good contacts and resources from your PE advisory group, including doctors and parents, who can support your message and add credibility to your cause.

• Once the local media cover an event, the national media may become interested. Don't be afraid to contact the national media directly if you think that you have a big story. Of course, you'll need to work with your administration, including your school district's communications director, on all major media activities, but rest assured that your school district will be happy to help you promote positive news about your program. PE4life can also help you get your story out to the national media.

• Use the sample press release located in appendix B and in the PE4life Academy section of www.pe4life.org to help you in your media relations efforts.

Develop your PE's program mission statement. (See chapter 8 for more details.)

_____

_____

_____

Create a list of key messages about PE in general and your program in particular.

_____

_____

_____

Create a list of individuals, groups, and organizations you want to reach with your messages. (In the first set of blank lines, identify at least three potential partners in each target area, and in the following lines, list key messages for each.)

Parents

_____

_____

_____

_____

_____

_____

Administrators and teachers

_____

_____

_____

_____

_____

Extended community (e.g., businesses [CEOs of corporations], civic leaders, and community organizations)

_____

_____

_____

_____

_____

_____

Medical community

_____

_____

_____

From *PE4life: Developing and Promoting Quality Physical Education,* by PE4life, 2007, Champaign, IL: Human Kinetics.

Media

_____

_____

_____

_____

_____

Determine how you want to initially engage the leaders in each of these target groups.

Parents

_____

_____

Administrators and teachers

_____

_____

Extended community

_____

_____

Medical community

_____

_____

Media

_____

_____

List possible roles for members of your community-based PE advisory group.

_____

_____

List potential newsworthy items, events, and activities related to your PE program.

_____

_____

_____

(continued)

Action Plan Worksheet   *(continued)*

List local media to present newsworthy items.

Newspapers: _____

Television stations: _____

Radio stations: _____

Magazines: _____

Other: _____

Take the Next Steps

What are your priorities for the following time frames?

Next six months	First year
_____	_____
_____	_____
_____	_____

Step 2: Implementation Plan

Task	Who is responsible?	When will it be completed?

Document the Results

What results did you see at the following times?

Six months

_____

_____

_____

One year

_____

_____

_____

Two years

_____

_____

_____

From *PE4life: Developing and Promoting Quality Physical Education,* by PE4life, 2007, Champaign, IL: Human Kinetics.

Pinpoint Funding Opportunities

Launch Your Fund-Raising Plan

The issue of adequate funding is universally cited as one of the biggest barriers to developing quality physical education programs. Some of the nation's most effective physical education programs, however, are located in schools with little in the way of allocated funds for physical education.

So how do they do it? With creativity and a steadfast commitment to making their PE4life Programs successful!

Start With the School District Budget

As you begin developing your PE4life Program, estimate how much each of your proposed changes will cost, prioritize your needs, and then look first within your school district for funding.

In some cases, if the items can be justified as curricular needs, the district will cover the cost. Likewise, many school districts and schools allocate funding in other areas, such as technology, that could be shifted in part to improve physical education programs (e.g., heart rate monitors, pedometers, and fitness software). By becoming a strong advocate for your program and by effectively using the equipment that you've purchased through school funds, you can position your program to receive more funding through the regular school budget. For example, the use of technology will allow physical education teachers and the program to be more accountable for results. You'll have the data to demonstrate for key stakeholders (e.g., school board members, administrators, fellow teachers, and parents) the positive effect that physical education has had on students.

Present your needs to the administration in a positive light. For example, heart rate monitors can have a tremendous effect on a physical education program. This reliable way to measure and evaluate student effort also motivates students to improve their fitness and activity levels. Measurement with heart rate monitors also levels the playing field so that every student can succeed and earn good grades in physical education, not just the athletically inclined. Teachers can carry a laptop or PDA into the gym or out on the field, allowing them to store data instantaneously. Administrators want to do what is best for students.

Research the benefits of quality, daily PE (see the introduction for a start and then explore appendix B) and put together a proposal that shows how new technology will help students attain those benefits. Remember, PE purchases are lifetime investments. Consider approaching the people in the district who are responsible for ordering technology for the district. Their budgets are typically larger than the budgets within departments at individual schools. By presenting compelling evidence about the effectiveness

"Many people think because we are in a suburban school district, we have an abundance of money for physical education. In reality, we have a $1,000 supply budget for approximately 1,000 students at the middle school—$1 per student. We've had to use creative measures to purchase all of the fitness-related equipment in our fitness center—no tax dollars have been used from our PE budget."

Phil Lawler,
PE4life Academy director,
Naperville, Illinois

of technology in physical education, you may be able to persuade decision makers to spend technology dollars on heart rate monitors, health-related fitness-testing computer technology, and even pedometers.

Even if you're able to squeeze some money out of the school district's budget to make incremental changes, this sum is unlikely to be enough for all the innovative things that you'll want to do with your program. At this point, you'll need to pursue some creative fund-raising for your program. Consider some of the following avenues to fund your new initiatives.

Ask Parent Organizations for Help

Most districts have parent groups that raise money to supplement what the district is already providing. If parents think that a program is important enough, they will come up with creative ways to fund it.

Remember that you need to connect with all parents. Raising money for physical education is different from raising money for athletics teams. For example, if your students need more equipment for building muscular strength and endurance, ask for equipment for a fitness center or a wellness club, not a weight room. Convey to all students the value of resistance training throughout life. Always try to communicate that your interest is in comprehensive health and wellness for every child in the school, not a program for the elite few.

Although you should differentiate raising money for physical education from raising money for athletics teams, be creative in building alliances with the various parent athletics booster clubs. Consider combining efforts to raise money for equipment that both your physical education program and the athletics teams can use.

Research Grants That May Assist Your Cause

Grants are available from a variety of sources, including the U.S. Department of Education, the National Institutes of Health, the Centers for Disease Control and Prevention, state governments, and private foundations. Specifically, the Department of Education's Carol M. White PEP grant program has awarded average grants of $200,000 to $400,000 to school districts and individual schools. All schools have an equal chance to receive the grants, with no advantages extended to wealthier school districts. By researching best practices and planning to make major changes in your program

that are in line with those best practices, you'll have a better chance to receive grant funding. You can visit the PE4life Web site (www.pe4life.org) to find grant opportunities (see also appendix B in this book). When applying for grants make sure that you write in measurable outcomes. This element is key to securing grant money. Fitnessgram, a tool that uses scientifically researched criteria, is often used as part of a grant request. Visit www.fitnessgram.net and click on Reference Guide to learn the appropriate uses of this tool. You can use other tools such as heart rate monitors and pedometers to show increased activity levels among students as the result of an improved physical education program.

The PE4life Web site provides not only a list of foundations and grant opportunities but also useful information on creative funding. In addition, the PE4life Web site provides an area to exchange ideas and questions with others across the World Wide Web. To find other sites with hidden gems on fund-raising, browse through the links on the site to other physical education organizations. Visit www.pe4life.org for all this and other information.

The Titusville program is unique due to the speed in which the change to a fitness-based program occurred and also due to the immediate local support received both in word and in action. After visiting Phil's program, within a span of two years we had heart rate monitors for all teachers; Tri-Fit systems in place at the middle school and high school; fitness centers with exercise equipment; and interactive video games in place at both the middle school and high school. Year three was when we won a PEP grant and updated all equipment and installed climbing walls in all buildings. Our district put over $100,000 into the PE program prior to the PE grant being awarded. The highlight of all of this occurred when our district instituted a change in the amount of PE our students receive. In a time where PE is under the knife to be eliminated or cut back, the Titusville Area School District *increased* the amount of PE time for high school students. Our high school students now have *daily* PE, during all four years of high school, and that is required for one full credit each year. We changed the entire school schedule to enable this to happen. In addition to this we instituted a kindergarten PE program. Prior to the 2004–05 school year, we had no PE for kindergarten students. We now have *daily* PE for these students also.

Tim McCord,
PE4life Academy director,
Titusville, Pennsylvania

the cost of building first-rate gyms in the new elementary schools. The physical education program uses the new gyms during the day, and the park district uses them at night. A similar example is in Grundy Center, Iowa, where the high school serves as a fitness center for the community. In both cases, the end solution proved to be a great way of pulling the school and community together. Consider other local community organizations that could benefit from such a relationship.

Explore Opportunities Through Community Activity Clubs

Look to other activity-oriented clubs in your community to see whether any working relationships could be forged. For example, a running club may be willing to help raise money for heart rate monitors for your school to help produce new community runners. Or the local square dance club might donate a CD player and CDs to help you teach potential members of their club. Perhaps a cycling club would raise money for bikes and helmets. The tennis club might donate used rackets and balls. Think creatively about incentives that you can provide to area clubs to work with your school. After all, isn't physical education class the best place for children to learn about various sports and other physical activities?

Tap Into Local Fitness Centers for Equipment Donation

Although you may not have the funds to buy new equipment for your school, local fitness centers and hospitals are often willing to donate used equipment. Also, consider approaching businesses that sell fitness equipment; they might, for example, donate an exercise bike that they've used for display purposes to help attract buyers. The bottom line is this: Don't be afraid to ask. Creativity knows no bounds!

For more fund-raising ideas and lists, visit these Web sites:

www.pe4life.org

www.aahperd.org/naspe

www.pecentral.com

www.pelinks4u.org

Scout Out Local Businesses and Service Organizations

All local businesses will benefit from a healthy and active population in their community. But think in particular about businesses in your community that are fitness or athletics oriented, such as health clubs. Or consider organizations such as hospitals and insurance companies that have an interest and investment in community well-being (see the Owensboro, Kentucky, example in chapter 2).

Likewise, look for community partners who have similar needs. For example, the school district in Champaign, Illinois, needed to build two elementary schools, and the park district needed to expand its facilities for its basketball leagues. The two got together and split

Collaborate With a Local University

Universities require professors to write grant applications. Contact the chair of the education department or physical education program at your local university and inquire about opportunities to work together to obtain grant money. By collaborating with a local university, you may find funding for training, equipment, or fitness assessment. You might also collaborate on research projects to help build evidence for the effectiveness of your program.

Learn From Local Athletics Organizations and Other Clubs in Your Community

The athletics programs at your school, as well as club sports teams and other activity clubs in your community, are often masters at fundraising. Pick the brains of the leaders of these groups for fund-raising ideas applicable to your program.

Remember: What Comes Around Goes Around

The first principle in creative funding is to recognize that you can't just hold out your hand and expect money. Look for ways to give back to those who donate money, equipment, or time to your program. For example, you might have your high school students spend a Saturday teaching soccer and fitness skills to first- and second-graders in exchange for physical education donations from the team's parents. Perhaps the local downtown business association would provide a donation to your program in exchange for a day of work by you and your students to spruce up the downtown area. Reciprocation not only helps raise funds but also builds positive relationships with members of the community.

List your fund-raising objectives and goals.

_____

_____

_____

Brainstorm potential fund-raising targets in each of the following areas.

School district (e.g., board members, administrators, teachers, technology coordinators)

_____

_____

Parent organizations

_____

_____

Local businesses

_____

_____

Community service organizations

_____

_____

Foundations and grants

_____

_____

Community activity clubs

_____

_____

Local fitness centers and health clubs

_____

_____

_____

From *PE4life: Developing and Promoting Quality Physical Education,* by PE4life, 2007, Champaign, IL: Human Kinetics.

Local universities and colleges

_____

_____

_____

Medical community

_____

_____

_____

Other potential sources

_____

_____

_____

Who is in charge of the technology budget and grant money in your school district? Do you know how to contact this person?

_____

_____

_____

Is there a local nonprofit association in your community that you could ask for help regarding foundations and grants?

_____

_____

_____

Have you heard of an organization within your community that has been awarded a grant? What can you do to learn from them?

_____

_____

_____

From a fund-raising perspective, how can you position your program as a "health and wellness partner" in the minds of the local medical community (e.g., hospitals, medical groups, and so on)?

_____

_____

_____

Who in your PE advisory group could head a fund-raising committee for the physical education program?

_____

_____

_____

(continued)

From _PE4life: Developing and Promoting Quality Physical Education,_ by PE4life, 2007, Champaign, IL: Human Kinetics.

Action Plan Worksheet   *(continued)*

Take the Next Steps

What are your priorities for the following time frames?

Next six months

_____

_____

_____

First year

_____

_____

_____

Step 3: Implementation Plan

Task	Who is responsible?	When will it be completed?

Document the Results

What results did you see at the following times?

Six months

_____

_____

_____

One year

_____

_____

_____

Two years

_____

_____

_____

From *PE4life: Developing and Promoting Quality Physical Education,* by PE4life, 2007, Champaign, IL: Human Kinetics.

CHAPTER 4

Get Equipped

Creating the Physical Foundation for Your PE4life Program

Of course, one of the primary goals of your PE4life Program is to get students moving. Physical education professionals and administrators must work together to determine the best way to facilitate the new program. Expecting to build a fitness center in the near term may not be reasonable. To get started correctly, however, you must think creatively about the best way to use your facilities and equipment.

Getting Started With Creating the Physical Space

Most schools have athletics facilities such as gymnasiums, fields, and weight rooms. But these facilities may not provide enough space for a well-rounded, quality physical education program. Search out places within the school such as an empty classroom or multipurpose room that could serve as a training ground for your program until a more suitable option becomes available. Lack of facilities should never be an excuse for not developing a PE4life Program.

Making It Happen in the Blue Valley School District

Representatives of the Blue Valley West (Kansas) High School, in the metro Kansas City area, attended the PE4life Academy in Naperville, Illinois, in October 2003. Inspired and motivated, they returned home and immediately went to work on creating their own PE4life Program. They quickly made tremendous progress. By late summer 2004 they had transformed their physical education program. Consider the following:

- They have a small fitness center that includes three treadmills, two elliptical trainers, two stair climbers, two bikes, one recumbent bike, three ski exercise machines, a couple of health riders, and some lightweight equipment. Most of the equipment was obtained by donation. They have talked to their parent–teacher organization about funding five more upright bikes and received a positive response. They rotate 28 students through the fitness center at one time.

- They dedicated a room next to their gym as their Tri-Fit testing center. The center contains Tri-Fit testing stations, bike ergometers, blood pressure cuffs, body composition scales, and a laser printer, and was repainted over the summer.

- The Blue Valley West PE staff conducted a staff development presentation for the entire Blue Valley West faculty, highlighting their new PE4life Program and giving tips to fellow teachers on how they could improve their personal fitness levels. They gave pedometers to faculty members after the presentation. This presentation helped boost faculty excitement about the school's new physical education program.

- Blue Valley West expanded its PE course offerings and rotates its classes every two weeks to give students exposure to more activities. New life-style-type activities include kayaking, yoga, Pilates, and tennis.

Perhaps the greatest change that the Blue Valley West PE team incorporated was adding new technology to its program. It greatly enhanced its technology tools by applying for school district technology funds. It received a large award and bought 40 E-600 heart rate monitors, five Polar handheld Companion pocket PC fitness tools (with the Tri-Fit fitness assessment system), and a Tanita body composition testing scale.

Nearby, Blue Valley Northwest High School is demonstrating that the use of technology-standardized fitness tests and the PE4life approach to physical education can motivate at-risk students that might otherwise dread, or be intimidated by, PE class. At Blue Valley, these students are developing a lifelong commitment to an active lifestyle. "This technology allows each student to participate regardless of their athletic ability . . . no child is left behind. It also encourages and reinforces the concept of self-responsibility," says Jean Drennan, a Blue Valley Northwest PE teacher.

"The technology justifies why we want our students to be active and healthy. Without the technology, students don't have any idea of what their individual health status is. . . . We have the students use their assessment data to plan exercise programs and set goals. The data is valid and reliable, so this is a positive to students, parents, and teachers," says Drennan.

Blue Valley West PE teacher Terry Flynn added, "We're running a comparative report for the kids, looking at their pre- and posttests on the Tri-Fit system, and we'll have them make an individual fitness plan as part of their final exam. We're also sending a five-page report home to the parents of each student detailing their progress on the various fitness components. All in all, we're well on our way to implementing a quality PE4life Program."

What Is the Ideal Environment for a PE4life Program?

Once you've raised the bar for quality, daily physical education, a fitness center must become a priority. At the middle and high school levels, a fitness center will be an integral part of your PE4life Program. Indeed, the value of a fitness center goes far beyond that of just a traditional weight room for athletes. A fitness center provides activities for the health and wellness of all children.

A comprehensive fitness center combines all the elements of cardiovascular endurance, aerobic capacity, flexibility, and strength. Besides weight-lifting machines, consider including treadmills, elliptical trainers, and stationary bicycles connected to video games in your fitness center. Some innovative centers are encompassing the idea of adventure education—think rock-climbing walls, high ropes, obstacle courses, and more. And, of course, technological tools such as heart rate monitors, pedometers, and fitness software are part of an ideal fitness center environment.

Where Does Basic PE Equipment Fit Into the Equation?

In moving toward a PE4life physical Program, adequate and safe equipment must be available for all students. There should never be a shortage of equipment. Simply put, quality physical education cannot be delivered if students have to stand in line waiting for equipment to participate.

A physical education teacher must not settle for a $200 budget for equipment. To advocate for quality physical education, teachers, parents, and administrators must demand an adequate supply of quality, safe equipment. If sufficient equipment is not available, the ultimate losers are the children. If school budgets are rigid, advocates must explore creative avenues to acquire equipment. Perhaps innovative programs can be developed with school athletics teams or the local parks and recreation department.

Do I Need Both an Aerobics Program and a Resistance Training Program?

A program that develops aerobic capacity alone does not constitute a well-rounded fitness program, nor will weights alone deliver good results. A quality program must incorporate both fitness elements. Resistance training at the middle and high school levels is extremely important. To be efficient movers, we must be stronger. Stronger muscles help us avoid injuries, burn calories more efficiently, build bone density, and fight osteoporosis. Resistance training is important for adolescents and is an integral component of lifetime health and wellness.

What Should My Priorities Be in Terms of Acquiring the Right Equipment?

As we have already learned, lack of resources is often cited as a reason for failing to implement PE4life Programs. But if you prioritize your needs, you can have the equipment that you need for a quality PE4life Program in just a few years.

Each school district must make decisions about facilities and equipment purchases based on the unique priorities, resources, and needs of individual schools. A PE4life Program, however, should never wait for school-based funding. Work with your PE advisory group to develop a three- to five-year plan for an ideal PE4life Program. Prioritize your goals for new equipment and facilities (see chapter 1 for more information on developing short- and long-term goals). As you begin to embrace PE4life principles in your program, we recommend that you consider the following:

• *Acquire heart rate monitors.* (See chapters 5 and 6 for more information on the benefits of heart rate monitors.) We strongly recommend that you acquire a full set of heart rate monitors so each student in a class has one to use, but even a single heart rate monitor will help you educate students about its use to gauge effort.

• *Ensure you have adequate sports equipment (balls, mats, jump ropes, and the like) to maximize participation.* As mentioned earlier, no student should have to stand around waiting for equipment to free up in order to get moving.

• *Invest in assessment testing equipment and software.* PE4life Academies incorporate hardware and software tools that involve and motivate students with comprehensive fitness assessments. These types of tools also allow educators to design custom exercise and nutrition plans to help students of all abilities reach their individual goals with the knowledge to sustain lifetime fitness and activity. Fitnessgram (see www.fitnessgram.net) is an inexpensive tool to evaluate health-related fitness and helps you assess student progress based on health and wellness standards rather than

athletics standards. It also provides individualized reports for both students and parents, in addition to providing statistical reports. Tri-Fit is a comprehensive software program, including equipment, that allows you to incorporate information gathered from Fitnessgram, perform complete fitness assessments, and design custom exercise and nutrition plans for students of all abilities (see chapter 6 for more information on assessment testing equipment and software).

• *Pursue equipment for adventure education.* As we'll explore in chapter 6, adventure education and team-building exercises are becoming important components of many PE programs. If you're interested in incorporating a rock-climbing wall into your facilities, do your homework. Research the benefits, learn how climbing ties into national PE standards, work with an accredited company to build the wall, and examine staff training needs and liability issues.

Building a Fitness Center

Integrating cardiovascular and weight-training equipment into a fitness center at your school is one of the best ways to demonstrate the benefits of daily physical activity. Introducing students to the proper use of this equipment and the value of cardio and resistance training has lifelong benefits; the local health club may become a regular destination for students throughout their lives. And building a fitness center doesn't always mean investing a lot of money. Look for creative ways to acquire equipment, including donations from health clubs (future destinations for our students), recycled equipment, and partnerships with sporting goods manufacturers and dealers.

Of course, do not forget the fee-free outdoors. Although not all neighborhoods are safe enough, when possible, walking and distance running can be a base of a cardiovascular program. Many communities have regular running and walking events where the goal is often to finish even at a modest pace. Participation in these events can provide wonderful lifelong learning experiences.

Experiential Learning and Adventure Education

The theory behind experiential learning dates back to the beginning of civilization. It is a belief that true learning occurs by doing practical hands-on activities. The thinking is that participation in unfamiliar activities with a group of people will lead a person to experience personal growth. If the activity is difficult and forces the group to accomplish the task by means of cooperation, communication, and experimentation, true learning takes place. If somehow the challenges can be repeatedly reconfigured, the skills that people utilize become familiar tools.

Therefore, the purpose of adventure education–type curriculum (see appendix C for examples) is to engage students in many different and challenging activities. The best activities are those that foster cooperation, communication, planning, trust, a sense of team, and risk taking all at the same time. Once the task has been completed, a debriefing by the group is a key element to the learning process. During the debriefing, students reflect on the skills needed by the group and individual skills that were necessary to complete the task. Debriefing allows students to express verbally to the group what was learned and what feelings were emitted as a result of participation in the activity. It's the hope that students will carry the experience gained from each activity to new challenges in other situations in their lives that might have similar circumstances. Learning takes place because new information is integrated both intellectually and kinesthetically.

Problem solving is what has moved civilization forward throughout the centuries. The more difficult the problem, the greater the amount of knowledge that is ultimately gained. Trial and error is what put man on the moon. Adventure education is a great problem-solving learning tool.

Adventure education also adds the element of risk into the learning process. The risk can be either real or perceived. Learning to deal with fears and succeeding will allow students to face difficult tasks more effectively in the future. Even when students are not successful at completing a task, learning takes place if proper debriefing occurs. Adventure education takes place on elements like rock-climbing walls, high-ropes courses, and low-ropes courses. Skills such as communication, trust, problem solving, cooperation, and risk taking are developed during adventure education activities.

One of the newest forms of orienteering that uses physical activity and technology is geocaching (see the *Journal of Physical Education, Recreation & Dance,* September 2005, p. 28, "Geocaching: 21st Century Hide and Seek," by Barbara Schlatter and Amy Hurd). Students use GPS systems to locate hidden "treasures," which are inexpensive items placed in a waterproof container and hidden in various locations (usually outdoors). Many adults enjoy this activity and it can be easily incorporated into a physical education curriculum.

These are the skills that corporate America is looking for in their workers. Companies spend thousands of dollars on this type of training. Schools can achieve true-life learning by including experiential learning and adventure education activities. It's been one of the most popular and successful initiatives in our PE4life Program in Naperville.

Paul Zientarski,
Physical Education Department chair,
Naperville, Illinois, Central High School

A Blueprint for Making the Most Out of Your Current Situation: Grundy Center, Iowa

Although there is no perfect situation in teaching, you can create futuristic programs regardless of your circumstances. As I was developing a vision of "Energizing and Educating for Healthy Lifestyles," our gymnasium was housed in the basement of a 70-year-old building. When the gym floors wore out, our school board purchased a gym floor that had been rescued from a building destroyed by fire. With the help of community members, I formed teams that cleaned and restored the boards and built the new gym floor. I spent the summer painting the gym and organizing skilled volunteers to help build a fitness area for our students.

Several years later, a school bond issue was passed, and we built a new elementary school. The gym design was a community effort that allowed input from many sources, including me, as the physical education instructor. This collaboration resulted in a truly effective teaching environment that today includes many child-centered learning ideas:

- My office is central with windows for two-way viewing.
- Restrooms and drinking fountains are inside the gym so that no child leaves the teaching and learning setting.
- Our gym is situated within the elementary complex so that no one walks through at any time to distract our students' attention from their lesson.
- Gravionic bars are built into the walls for decompression exercises that build strength and develop positive posture alignment.
- Equipment and heart rate monitor storage areas are built into the facility design.
- A unique low-ceiling tiled area between my office and the gymnasium provides a space conducive to instruction, as well as space for heart rate banners and charts to promote what is happening in PE.
- Personal spaces are painted on the gym floor and numbers are painted on the wall to aid in class management protocols.
- In 2002–2003, our student senate initiative provided us with a rock-climbing wall in our gymnasium.

Rick Schupbach,
PE4life Academy director,
Grundy Center, Iowa

List your facility and equipment goals and objectives.

_____

_____

_____

List potential facility modifications or additions to your current structure.

_____

_____

_____

List your equipment priorities.

_____

_____

_____

What are your PE technology tool priorities?

_____

_____

_____

Consider innovative ways to get the equipment you need (e.g., community partnerships, in-kind services, and so on).

_____

_____

_____

Consider innovative ways to get the facilities you need (e.g., co-ops with the local parks and recreation department).

_____

_____

_____

In the near term, how can you accomplish your health and wellness goals without the facilities and equipment you desire?

_____

_____

_____

(continued)

From *PE4life: Developing and Promoting Quality Physical Education,* by PE4life, 2007, Champaign, IL: Human Kinetics.

Take the Next Steps

What are your priorities for the following time frames?

Next six months

_____

_____

_____

First year

_____

_____

_____

Step 4: Implementation Plan

Task	Who is responsible?	When will it be completed?

Document the Results

What results did you see at the following times?

Six months

_____

_____

_____

One year

_____

_____

_____

Two years

_____

_____

_____

CHAPTER 5

Design Your PE4life Program

Implementation of the PE4life Approach

Now that you've evaluated the physical space and equipment requirements for your PE4life Program, let's look at the nuts and bolts—what innovative new instruction, activities, and adventures will you incorporate as you develop your PE4life Program?

Remember, many of your key stakeholders—administrators, school board members, parents, and community leaders—may have had bad experiences in "gym class" as they grew up, and consequently may believe that PE is not needed. Others may take it for granted that PE is the same as it's always been and don't see its importance to our children's health and wellness. You must sell the fact that you're

creating something new, innovative, and exciting—that you're helping students become physically active for life.

In this section we'll explore the components of a standard PE4life Program and provide examples of activities that you can adapt for your school's PE4life Program.

Components of a PE4life Program

Before we explore how to design your program, we want to reemphasize the basic principles that every PE4life Program demonstrates or is working toward.

As described on the PE4life program application, PE4life Programs combine today's best practices in physical education to inspire and educate all students about the vital importance of lifetime physical activity and fitness. PE4life Programs incorporate cardiovascular fitness, muscular strength and endurance, and team building and adventure education within the curriculum; utilize technology and individualized student assessments; and encourage involvement with local health, medical, and business communities.

How Does a PE4life Program Differ From the Old Way of Doing Things?

The physical education that many of us grew up with focused simply on improving or measuring sport skills—learning how to throw a ball better, seeing who could run the fastest, or learning how to beat the other team. This emphasis on athletics skills and competition caused many children who weren't interested in sports, or couldn't succeed in them, to turn away from physical activity. Many viewed "gym class" as 40 minutes to be endured; others truly dreaded it. Many children do not enjoy sports or competition. Yet these students have the same physical fitness and health needs as our most competitive and skilled athletes.

A PE4life Program features cooperative as well as competitive sports. It introduces lifetime sports and physical activities. It eliminates practices that humiliate students. And it assesses students on their progress in reaching personal physical activity and fitness goals. A PE4life Program exposes students to the fun and long-term benefits of movement—it's that simple. Exercise does not need to be painful to be beneficial, but it does take education, time, and effort.

"This is physical education of the future available right now. The way the PE4life Program is structured, it's almost like each student has his or her own personal trainer."

Paul O'Palka,
past director,
community affairs,
Highmark Blue Cross/Blue Shield

Does a PE4life Program Eliminate Competition and Sports?

No! Teaching children the value of gaining or improving sport skills is an important part of PE4life. What is different is the degree of emphasis. Competition doesn't need to be a point of emphasis in physical education because the competitive athlete can participate in after-school sports programs. Physical education is the arena for all children, regardless of athletic ability, to reap the benefits of exercise and movement. Simply put, competition can be a part of your PE4life Program, but it shouldn't be the primary part.

Let's face it; one of the greatest competitions any of us will ever face is the challenge of maintaining our health, and in this competition, the outcome is more critical than the result in any game or contest we play. The rising rate of obesity clearly shows that too many of us are losing that contest. PE4life helps train young people to be winners in the lifelong game of health and wellness.

How Can You Adapt Traditional Sports Activities Based on PE4life Principles?

As we've mentioned earlier, adopting PE4life principles doesn't mean forgoing sports and other traditional PE activities. But it does mean thinking about how you can adapt those activities to involve and reward all students, not just the athletically inclined. When looking at your basketball, soccer, softball, hockey, and other sports lessons, look for ways to increase overall movement. Find ways to ensure that all students can be involved. Think about how students can continue enjoying and benefiting from these sports, or specific aspects of these sports, over a lifetime. For example, one school changed its approach to soccer by breaking the class into small teams and eliminating the goalie. The result? Students are always moving on the field, not just waiting around for the ball to come their way. They are focused on staying active and having fun rather than on winning or losing.

Successful PE4life Programs modify team sports to get more students involved and moving. For example, 11v11 soccer and football become 4v4. Basketball is 3v3 instead of 5v5. More action occurs, and more students have a chance to use and develop sport skills.

"Our physical education program at Deer Path has changed. We have made a shift from a skill-based curriculum to a fitness-based curriculum. This does not mean we have taken sports out of the curriculum, but we've modified their concepts to be fitness oriented."

Bob Van Kast,
Wellness Department chairperson,
Deer Path Middle School East,
Lake Forest, Illinois

What's the Role of Having Fun in PE4life Programs?

Obviously, we want the PE experience to be fun for students. But staying fit is hard work, and that means that students are not always going to perceive PE as fun. If our ultimate goal is only to make physical education fun, then who or what will make it fun for students after they leave school? Our goal should be to develop intrinsic motivation and good habits—to instill in our students the drive to stay fit for a lifetime.

"It's not our job to make students be fit, but rather to provide them with the information and lead them to an awareness of the value and importance of taking care of themselves. We don't practice the traditional sports approach, but rather urge individual goal setting. It's more of a fitness club mentality, promoting individualized programs and offering students the chance to take themselves as high as they can. We strive for an end result of imparting an intrinsic desire to be fit, along with the knowledge of how to accomplish that, something they can then carry with them throughout their lives."

Paul Zientarski, Physical Education
Department chair, Naperville,
Illinois, Central High School

Where Does Nutrition Education Fit Into the PE4life Model?

Just as teaching our students the benefits of movement is so important, teaching the message of good nutrition is also vital. You may perceive that nutrition is a fairly complex subject; however, there are just two important equations we need to impart to our students:

> A well-balanced diet + physical activity = a healthy lifestyle
>
> Energy balance equation regarding body weight (energy in = energy out)

When considering the energy in = energy out equation, keep in mind the following:

- When energy in (calories eaten) is equal to energy out (calories burned during physical activity), your body weight is stable.
- When energy in is greater than energy out, then you will gain body weight.
- When energy in is less than energy out, then you will lose body weight.

These simple equations are so important to convey. Overall, our society struggles to bal-

Physical Inactivity Is the Primary Culprit

Although sound nutrition is undoubtedly an important component of children's overall health, the primary cause of the childhood obesity epidemic today is that children aren't getting enough exercise. In recent months, we've seen an increase in the number of studies pointing to physical inactivity as the primary culprit in our kids' "battle of the bulge."

The problem starts with toddlers. A study published in *Lancet* in January 2004 found that 3-year-olds today consume slightly fewer calories than did the 3-year-olds of 25 years ago. The problem is that physical activity levels of toddlers have dropped dramatically.

A lack of physical activity remains the primary culprit through the teen years, despite a slight increase in caloric intake. Recent findings by researchers at San Diego State University and the School of Medicine at the University of California at San Diego found that the lack of physical activity was the most significant risk factor contributing to obesity in 11- to 15-year-olds.

The physical inactivity epidemic is worsening. University of Missouri biomedical professor Frank Booth has labeled the problem "sedentary death syndrome."

"Inactivity kills. Everyone knows exercise is good for them, but many don't realize it's a matter of life and death," according to Booth.

Consider a few alarming statistics: Ten times as many children had type 2 diabetes in 2002 as in 1997. The incidence of high blood pressure in teenagers is steadily on the rise. Nearly 22 percent of preschool children in the United States today can be defined as overweight, and 10 percent are obese.

Making this picture even uglier is the fact that while the physical fitness and health of our kids have been steadily declining, the number of physical education classes in our schools have been dropping as well. The return of quality, daily physical education can help reverse these disturbing trends by inspiring active, healthy lifestyles.

As Dr. Kenneth Cooper, known as the father of aerobics, says, "If we're going to halt the childhood obesity epidemic and get our kids on a path toward physical fitness, one area that must improve dramatically is our country's physical education system."

Dr. Kenneth Reed, author,
PE4life "Blueprint for Change"

ance calories consumed with calories burned. Teaching the checks-and-balances philosophy early on will be one of the best gifts we can give our children as they grow.

Look for creative ways to fit nutrition education into your curriculum. Help students understand that maintaining a healthy weight boils down to this one simple equation: balancing calories in with calories out. Illustrate this point by discussing the caloric content of several healthy and less healthy common food items, followed by showing students how many calories can be burned while performing specific physical activities. Further demonstrate this concept by exploring with students the nutrition software packages that are available to monitor caloric intake (see the nutrition section in appendix A).

Consider encouraging parents to become more involved in their child's health by organizing a parent group to work with food-service providers to develop ideas for offering healthier meal and snack options to students. It may mean teaming up with administrators and other teachers to evaluate the overall messages we are conveying to children about nutrition—from the food served in the cafeteria, to the treats we offer students during the holidays, to the activities conducted in health education classes. With the newly established requirement that school districts develop a local wellness policy, information and resources to assist school districts to meet or exceed the model guidelines are available to facilitate open discussions with parents, school administrators, and classroom teachers on how best to implement healthy food options. For ideas on nutrition education materials and tools, refer to the nutrition resources located in appendix A.

Finally, it's important to remember that our focus as physical educators is on cultivating active lifestyles in our students. It's also important to note that recent research has pinpointed physical inactivity as the primary culprit in the childhood obesity epidemic.

PE4life Activities

We've provided here some examples of how you can adopt a coordinated approach to curriculum development and incorporate activities in your program that embrace the core PE4life principles: involving all students, focusing on fitness and lifetime sports, using technology, and motivating children to embrace health and wellness for a lifetime.

Working with your end goal in mind, begin gathering input from as many resources as possible to develop an innovative curriculum. Include representatives from the elementary, middle, and high schools to develop a coordinated and holistic curriculum that teaches children the tenets of health and wellness throughout their school experience.

We also recommend that you reference the Physical Best program of the National Association for Sport and Physical Education (NASPE) for ideas on incorporating health-related fitness activities into your PE4life Program. Physical Best is a comprehensive health-related physical fitness education program which we believe strongly supports and complements the principles of PE4life. For more information on Physical Best, and NASPE's PIPEline Workshops, call NASPE at 800-213-7183, ext. 426, or visit www.HumanKinetics.com/physicalbest/index.cfm.

An additional program sponsored by NASPE is called NASPE Stars, a national recognition

program for outstanding K–12 physical education programs in the United States. Victor High School, in New York, was the recipient of this recognition for reorganizing its physical education program to offer units that included canoeing, kickboxing, rock climbing, self-defense for girls, cardio kickboxing, cross-country skiing, orienteering, rugby, dance, team handball, hydro fitness, in-line skating, tennis, and distance running. See Shelly Collins, "Striving for the Stars—the Victor High School Experience," *Strategies* January, February, 2006, p. 33.

SPARK programs (www.sparkpe.org) are award-winning, research-based curricula designed for physical education programs from early childhood through high school, including after-school initiatives.

Also, always use the description of a PE4life Program, which is given on the PE4life program application (see www.pe4life.org). The national standards of the National Association of Sport and Physical Education (NASPE) should provide a checks-and-balances tool as you consider your curriculum (see appendix B for NASPE guidelines).

Embracing PE4life in Grundy Center, Iowa

My passion for teaching physical education has led me to build a PE4life Program that I believe truly meets the needs of each of my students. The challenge is to continue to maintain and improve existing practices and ensure the program lives on long after I leave. Our administrators encouraged me to align my curriculum with our schools' collective vision to educate students in a way that will meet the needs of their future lifestyles. In fourth and fifth grade, I measure this outcome through having every student create "personal lifestyle prescriptions"—in other words, personal progress plans. My goal is to help students make healthy lifestyle choices they would not have selected unless I intervened.

Using a wide range of activities, unique class format design, technology, and interactive learning stations, Grundy Center has a program that addresses a different aspect and concept of lifestyle education each class period in grades 4 and 5. Students spend time designing personal lifestyle prescriptions, with several opportunities to revise and change their selections throughout the year. Continually participating in thought-provoking activities that introduce new options requires our students to challenge their thinking and choices. This process also encourages parents to take an active role in their child's health through helping the child work on obtaining their goals throughout the year.

Rick Schupbach,
PE4life Academy director,
Grundy Center, Iowa

Action Plan
W O R K S H E E T

How is your current PE program congruent with the PE4life philosophy?

_____

_____

_____

How does your current PE program differ from the PE4life philosophy?

_____

_____

_____

List the benefits of transitioning to a PE4life program.

_____

_____

_____

What new activities can you incorporate into your PE curriculum?

_____

_____

_____

How can you adapt your traditional sports activities to PE4life principles (e.g., small-sided teams)?

_____

_____

_____

Name three specific ways technology can advance the delivery of PE in your school.

_____

_____

_____

List three relatively easy and quick actions you could take right now toward becoming a PE4life program.

_____

_____

_____

How can you help students set personalized fitness goals?

_____

_____

_____

(continued)

From *PE4life: Developing and Promoting Quality Physical Education,* by PE4life, 2007, Champaign, IL: Human Kinetics.

Take the Next Steps

What are your priorities for the following time frames?

Next six months

_____

_____

_____

First year

_____

_____

_____

Step 5: Implementation Plan

Task	Who is responsible?	When will it be completed?

Document the Results

What results did you see at the following times?

Six months

_____

_____

_____

One year

_____

_____

_____

Two years

_____

_____

_____

Develop a Plan to Assess Success

Measuring Your ROI

Just as business managers evaluate their return on investment (ROI) to assess the success of a new venture, physical educators can productively think in terms of ROI in evaluating PE activities. How can we best measure our students' progress? Are the appropriate rubrics in place to assess the effectiveness of new activities? How will we make students accountable for their work in PE? How can we hold ourselves accountable as physical educators? How will we define success? (See chapter 10 for more details about assessment.)

> "The questions at the end of the day are: How did you do as a teacher? How did your students do? How did you measure it? How are you conveying that to your administrators, parents, and students?"
>
> *Beth Kirkpatrick, pioneering 20-year physical education instructor, PE4life Academy director, Grundy Center, Iowa*

In this section, we discuss the importance of formulating a plan to assess your students' progress, as well as the overall effectiveness of your PE4life Program.

Why Is Measuring Return on Investment Important in PE?

Just as teachers of math, English, and other disciplines are required to collect data to demonstrate growth in student learning, PE must embrace a sense of accountability if we want our programs to be equally valued. Let's face it: In education today, if something is to be respected, it must be tested. If we do not assess students in physical education, the class will not be valued as an integral part of the school's overall delivery.

> "It's a 3-D world: Data drive decisions. In PE, we haven't had the data, so we've been easy to drop or ignore."
>
> *Rick Schupbach, PE4life Academy director, Grundy Center, Iowa*

"In our community, the expectation for success is high. When we incorporated physical education into the GPA, the staff saw a dramatic impact on the students' attitudes toward physical education. Because it was given the same credit and value as math, science, and English, they finally realized it was as important as any other class they took. That awareness has led to better participation and cooperation by the students in class. The expectation now is that students will perform to the best of their ability in class, especially since we do not grade students on athletic skills but on effort and cooperation. Students with infirmities are now finding alternative activities, with the aid of their teacher, rather than not participating in class."

Paul Zientarski, Physical Education Department chair, Naperville (Illinois) Central High School

How Do We Determine Whether Our Efforts Are Effective?

Remember, a PE4life Program provides authentic, individualized assessment, including fitness testing and cognitive testing, as a meaningful part of the learning process. This type of assessment empowers students to value and oversee their personal lifetime fitness.

As you continue to refine and make changes to your program, you need to provide data that objectively measure improvement. You can measure your students' progress in several ways, including heart rate monitors and fitness software like the Fitnessgram (see figure 6.1 on page 52). Although you can't completely evaluate your PE4life Program simply by looking at fitness scores, they do serve as one baseline tool to measure improvement.

Sample Tools to Help You Measure Your ROI

Following are several examples of tools that can help you effectively measure your ROI and assess the progress of your students.

• *Heart rate monitors.* As we've discussed in other sections, heart rate monitors are serving as a springboard for change in PE4life Programs across the country. Here's what they can provide your program:

- Opportunity to test cardiovascular fitness compared with national norms
- Mechanism to push students safely to their maximum effort while monitoring their activity
- Way to evaluate the lessons taught after the class period
- Assessment of whether students are active in the areas that you think they are
- Ability to manage your time more effectively, for example, to know how much time was spent in instruction versus activity
- Portrait of individual accomplishment for the student as well as a measure of success for the teacher
- Tool for cross-curricular activities, offering students opportunities

to measure calorie expenditures, examine bar graphs, explore percentages, and use skills learned in other disciplines

- Way for students to understand how the heart works and gain more knowledge about their personal heart health

Think creatively about how you can introduce heart rate monitors into your PE4life Program. Is funding available in your budget? If not, can you tap into a school district budget for technology? Can you look outside the school for other sources of funding or donations? Chapter 3 provides detailed information on how you can help fund your PE4life Program.

- *Individual lifestyle prescription plans.* If you're embracing the 21st century PE and focusing on promoting lifetime heath and wellness, you must think creatively about ways to individualize the fitness experience. Think about providing a lifestyle prescription plan for each of your students. Using this approach,

students aren't competing against each other, but rather are measuring their success on a personal basis based on daily, weekly, and yearly progress. Fitnessgram and Activitygram provide excellent tools for getting started. Fitness for Life and Physical Best provide strategies for teaching students to do personal planning.

- *Cholesterol screening.* Screening your students for cholesterol is an example of an initiative on which you can work cooperatively with the medical community. To educate both students and parents about the importance of cholesterol screening, you and your medical partner can provide this service through physical education class. (Remember that you will likely need parental or guardian permission.) Tie in lessons about the effects of genetics, nutrition, and physical activity on cholesterol levels. Your local medical partner can help provide information. Don't let cost be a barrier—medical providers may welcome the opportunity for preventative action and might donate services.

How Heart Rate Monitors Served As a Lifeline for One PE4life Program

With the use of heart rate monitors, I give each student complete and continual feedback during cardiovascular testing. This helps motivate them to succeed. It also helps ensure the safety of the participants, as both the student and I know whether he or she is staying in the target heart rate zone. Students can make the necessary adjustments as a result of the constant feedback. I can also send a hard copy or paperless (e-mail) printout of the results to every parent.

I presented our school board with the results from our heart rate monitor usage, providing compelling, objective visual evidence that my fourth- and fifth-graders were in their target heart rate zone 90 percent of the time for at least 15 minutes during PE class during the year. Providing this and other types of data immediately

validated the importance of physical education and gave it instant credibility in the eyes of the board of education. In my mind, I'm convinced that PE will not be cut in our school because it would diminish the health of students. When someone asks why we need PE, I can say without reservation that each student's heart is gaining in cardiovascular endurance. I have evidence. If they want to cut PE, I want them to know they will be cutting the "heart" out of the child's education. With rising health care costs, we need to be preventive and proactive. Our lifestyle approach to PE is paramount to what we're doing as a profession.

Rick Schupbach,
PE4life Academy director,
Grundy Center, Iowa

FITNESSGRAM®

Your scores on all tests were in or above the Healthy Fitness Zone. Continue strength exercises and do flexibility exercises. Add aerobic activity most every day.

Instructor: Kathy Read

	Date	Height	Weight
Current:	09/20/2006	5' 5"	137 lbs

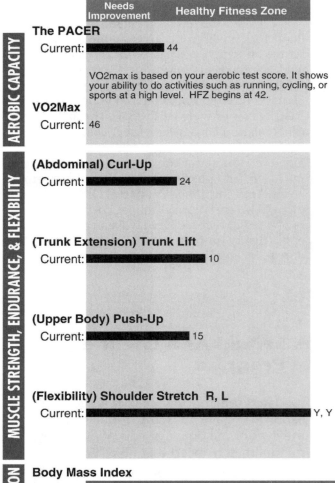

AEROBIC CAPACITY

The PACER
Current: 44

VO2max is based on your aerobic test score. It shows your ability to do activities such as running, cycling, or sports at a high level. HFZ begins at 42.

VO2Max
Current: 46

MUSCLE STRENGTH, ENDURANCE, & FLEXIBILITY

(Abdominal) Curl-Up
Current: 24

(Trunk Extension) Trunk Lift
Current: 10

(Upper Body) Push-Up
Current: 15

(Flexibility) Shoulder Stretch R, L
Current: Y, Y

BODY COMPOSITION

Body Mass Index

Healthy Fitness Zone	Needs Improvement
Very Low	

Current: 22.80

Being too lean or too heavy may be a sign of (or lead to) health problems.

MESSAGES

Although your aerobic capacity score is in the Healthy Fitness Zone now, you are not doing enough physical activity. Try to participate in moderate or vigorous aerobic activities 30 to 60 minutes at least 5 days each week to maintain your fitness.

Your abdominal, trunk, and upper-body strength are in the Healthy Fitness Zone. To maintain your fitness, be sure that your strength-training activities include resistance exercises for all of these areas. Abdominal and trunk exercises should be done 3 to 5 days each week. Strength activities for other parts of your body should be done 2 to 3 days each week.

Your flexibility is in the Healthy Fitness Zone. To maintain your flexibility, you should begin doing slow stretches 3 or 4 days each week, holding the stretch 20-30 seconds. Don't forget that you need to stretch all areas of the body.

Charlie, your body composition is in the Healthy Fitness Zone. Doing physical activity most days may help to maintain your level of body composition. You should also eat a healthy diet including more fruits and vegetables and fewer fats and sugars.

Healthy Fitness Zone for 13 year-old boys
The PACER = 41 - 83 laps
Curl-Up = 21 - 40 repetitions
Trunk Lift = 9 - 12 inches
Push-Up = 12 - 25 repetitions
Shoulder Stretch = Must be Yes on R & L
Body Mass Index = 15.10 - 23.00

ACTIVITY

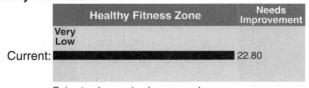

	Number of Days
On how many of the past 7 days did you participate in physical activity for a total of 30-60 minutes, or more, over the course of the day?	3
On how many of the past 7 days did you do exercises to strengthen or tone your muscles?	2
On how many of the past 7 days did you do exercises to loosen up or relax your muscles?	1

To be healthy and fit it is important to do some physical activity almost every day. Aerobic exercise is good for your heart and body composition. Strength and flexibility exercises are good for your muscles and joints.

Good job! You are doing some aerobic activity and strength and flexibility exercises. Additional vigorous aerobic activity would help to promote higher levels of fitness.

©2005 The Cooper Institute

Figure 6.1 Fitnessgram is an assessment tool that provides individualized feedback based on criteria-referenced standards associated with good health.

From FITNESSGRAM, © 2005 The Cooper Institute.

• *Fitness testing.* Assessing your students' overall fitness is one of the most important things that you can do for their overall health and wellness. Invest in technology that helps you assess cardiovascular fitness, muscular strength, muscular endurance, and body composition. Alternatively, collaborate with a local physical therapist or university exercise physiologist to conduct the testing for you. This approach is an excellent way to reach out to the community and adds validity to your outcomes.

• *Fitnessgram.* Fitnessgram is an inexpensive tool to evaluate cardiovascular fitness, muscular strength, muscular endurance, and body composition. A major benefit is that Fitnessgram helps you assess progress by health and wellness standards rather than by athletics standards. Fitnessgram is designed to provide individualized feedback to students and parents, while being used as an educational tool

by teachers. However, it can also be used for institutional testing (see page 91), and the data generated may provide direction for curriculum planning.

• Other fitness assessment software is available, such as the Tri-Fit assessment program and Microfit. The Tri-Fit system, currently licensed to include the Fitnessgram test, allows you to perform additional fitness assessments and design custom exercise and nutrition plans for students of all physical abilities. The system prints educational reports for students, progress and trend reports, class lists, and group summary reports to show improvement of a particular class or grade. The Tri-Fit program allows instructors to assess blood pressure, body weight, body composition, flexibility, cardiovascular fitness, strength, and many other measures.

• *Cognitive (knowledge) testing.* According to the National Association for Sport and Physical Education (NASPE), the intent of standard 2 of the National Standards for Physical Education is "facilitation of learners' ability to use cognitive information to understand and enhance motor skill acquisition and performance" (*Moving Into the Future: National Standards for Physical Education, Second Edition*, NASPE, 2004). The intent of standard 4 is "development of students' knowledge, skills, and willingness to accept responsibility for personal fitness, leading to an active, healthy lifestyle." One way to measure the achievement of these standards is to use

> Our entire PE curriculum is now solely based on individual effort. Not only do students know the hows, whats, and whys about physical activity, but they can also track their own daily and annual progress. The software we use provides reports on all the health-related components of fitness for each student. At BVNW High School this is done without any other specialized fitness equipment, a state-of-the-art facility, or a huge budget. Instead of rolling out the ball daily, teachers simply roll out the fitness technology equipment from the storage room for students to use in conjunction with their activities and games.
>
> *Jean Drennan,*
> *director of physical education,*
> *Blue Valley Northwest High School,*
> *Overland Park, Kansas*

cognitive (knowledge) testing. Dr. Weimo Zhu (University of Illinois) and his colleagues are currently developing a national physical education knowledge test that should be available in 2008. Currently the Fitness for Life program (Dr. Charles Corbin) offers cognitive tests for high school students and will have them available for middle school students in 2007. See www.fitnessforlife.org for more information and access to the Fitness for Life Test Bank. Also available at www.fitnessforlife.org is a student online study guide that can be used to create an electronic portfolio of student work. This program is available free to Fitness for Life adopters.

You can use these tests not only to assess the knowledge of students about health-related fitness but also to show the need for daily PE for reasons other than just physical activity. We can assure the nation that every child that goes through a public school with a PE4life Program will have the knowledge to take care of his or her health. Sport skills questions should probably not be included in these knowledge tests.

Another value of these tests is that they bolster the argument against students' use of waivers to avoid taking PE and they make a case for why we need daily PE. One could put the test in front of administrators and school boards and ask, "When are students going to learn this information if they do not learn it in daily PE?"

Research results can also help convince skeptics of the value of physical education. If you have a university in your community, you might approach professors in the physical education department about doing research at your school on the benefits of quality physical education.

What assessments are you currently employing to measure the health and wellness of your students?

_____

_____

_____

What is your grading philosophy in regard to effort versus skill level?

_____

_____

_____

What tools or indicators do you use to measure effort?

_____

_____

_____

Assess the accuracy, validity, and effectiveness of your current grading system.

_____

_____

_____

How can you use fitness scores to demonstrate accountability and promote the value of your program in the eyes of key targets (e.g., administrators, parents, teachers, and the like)?

_____

_____

_____

How can you incorporate "lifestyle prescription plans" into your current program?

_____

_____

_____

How might the use of fitness and cognitive health and wellness assessments, like the ones highlighted in chapter 6, change your approach to physical education?

_____

_____

_____

Have you brought brain research into your physical education program?

_____

_____

_____

(continued)

From *PE4life: Developing and Promoting Quality Physical Education,* by PE4life, 2007, Champaign, IL: Human Kinetics.

Take the Next Steps

What are your priorities for the following time frames?

Next six months

_____

_____

_____

First year

_____

_____

_____

Step 6: Implementation Plan

Task	Who is responsible?	When will it be completed?

Document the Results

What results did you see at the following times?

Six months

_____

_____

_____

One year

_____

_____

_____

Two years

_____

_____

_____

From *PE4life: Developing and Promoting Quality Physical Education,* by PE4life, 2007, Champaign, IL: Human Kinetics.

CHAPTER 7

Learn to Troubleshoot and Overcome Roadblocks

Overcoming Barriers

As you move forward with developing your PE4life Program, you're bound to encounter some barriers and roadblocks along the way. Don't let potential or real challenges set you back! Believe in your vision, cultivate strong allies, and be persistent but patient as you pave the way for change. In this section we identify some common challenges and how you can overcome them.

• *Perception: "PE is under-valued in my school."* Educators looking to implement PE4life Programs in their schools often cite the lack of respect given to physical education as the top challenge. Despite all the research that supports the value of daily exercise, old mind-sets regarding PE may make it difficult to effect positive change. High-stakes academic testing required by most states has pushed PE to the bottom of the priority list or squeezed it out altogether.

> "The key to addressing the value of PE is to answer the question, What am I teaching my child that's not only important for them today but also critical to the rest of their lives?"
>
> **Phil Lawler, PE4life Academy director, Naperville, Illinois**

That's where your team's advocacy efforts come into play. Use the resources presented in this book and do your research on the numerous positive effects of quality, daily PE. Discourage people from lumping PE in with other "special" courses held only once a week in some schools. Remember, PE is the only subject that is critical to long-term health! Look for the support of important allies, including members of the medical community, who can add instant credibility to your cause. Create an innovative but practical plan of action. Lean on your colleagues in your district, state, and across the country. Many of them have faced—and overcome—the very challenges confronting you now. Most important, believe in your vision and mission. You can change the perception of PE in your schools.

• *Perception: "We don't have the funds to make significant changes to our PE Program."* Funding is a major challenge for most schools. But some

of the most successful PE4life Programs across the country have identified creative ways to find funding outside their school's budget. We have provided many resources and examples in this manual. Build a strong case for your vision first. Then look for equipment donations, turn to parents' organizations for fund-raising opportunities, tap into local businesses, align with your medical community, and explore available grants. As you begin to make some positive changes in your PE program, you are simultaneously building a stronger case for receiving more funding in the future from the school budget.

• *Perception*: *"Our facilities aren't near enough to par to develop a PE4life Program."* A lack of facilities should never be an excuse for not providing a quality, daily PE program. If you feel that your school's gymnasium doesn't provide enough space for a quality physical education program, search out places within your school, such as an empty classroom or multipurpose room, that could serve as a training ground for your program until a more suitable option

How Daily Physical Education Can Be a Reality in Your School

In Titusville, Pennsylvania, Tim McCord and his PE4life advocates helped change the school-day schedule to provide daily physical education. Here's how they did it:

"The idea of daily PE was first suggested by the high school principal. He was pleased with the changes we had made to our program directly related to the PE4life Academy's model. He laid the groundwork with the school board, and I made the presentations at the public school board meeting, citing statistics on obesity and discussing brain research from Dr. John Ratey at Harvard and others. Here's how we restructured the school day to make way for daily PE:

1. Our normal school day consisted of eight periods with classes lasting 43 minutes. Travel time between classes was 5 minutes.

2. The first change was to move to a nine-period day by changing classes to 40 minutes. The principal thought the day would be better served by changing to nine periods, which would allow for daily PE and more flexibility in a student's schedule for electives. It would also allow PE to be a stand-alone class, meaning it would no longer be married, so to speak, to the science labs.

3. To make room for the extra period, the school day was extended by 12 minutes (still staying within the confines of the employee contract). Travel time between classes was cut in half to allow only 3 minutes.

4. At the time of the changes, we had five full-time physical education staff members. Today we have the same number of staff members. We accomplished the entire change without any cost to the district."

becomes available. The ultimate goal for your PE4life Program is to get students moving, so look for creative ways to make the most of your available space. Then, as your program grows in success, you'll be more likely to obtain the funding that you need to build new facilities, such as a fitness center.

• *Perception*: *"We don't have enough time in our school day for daily PE."* Responding to pressure to emphasize specific subject areas for high-stakes educational assessments, many schools are reducing or eliminating PE programs to focus on math, science, English, and other subjects. But multiple research studies are now showing that daily physical activity can have a positive effect on brain development and enhance academic performance in traditional academic subjects. If people believe that the school can't afford to set aside time for daily physical education, remind them that they can't afford not to.

Incorporate these messages into your advocacy efforts and be convinced that daily PE can be a reality in your school. Make the case for why daily PE is critical to children's health and wellness. Then work with your school's administrators to look for ways to restructure the school day to make room for daily PE, such as reducing travel time between classes, extending the school day by a few minutes, and adding an extra class period.

• *Perception*: *"I don't know how to change the mind-set of 'old-school' PE teachers."* As we've mentioned previously, some people are critical of the new way of looking at physical educa-

tion. Some believe that PE should be taught the way it has always been taught, based on a team sports model. Yes, athletics can provide benefits to many students. But remember, physical education should not target the athletically inclined; it's for all students and should benefit everyone. Demonstrate the progress in the total health and wellness of your students over weeks, months, and years. Make it clear that sports still have a place in daily PE4life Programs. Show critics how team sports can be modified to get all students involved and active. Invite doubters to attend a PE4life Academy to see 21st century PE in action for themselves. Before you know it, you'll see the mind-sets of these "old-school" PE believers begin to evolve.

• *Perception*: *"I don't know where to begin to gather the resources and information that I'll need."* This book is a good place to start building your knowledge of the benefits of quality, daily PE and ways to begin implementing a PE4life Program in your school. Check out the dozens of resources available at www.pe4life.org, including our "Blueprint for Change." Call your peers in the industry who have attended a PE4life Academy and have a PE4life Program in place, or are working toward one, to exchange ideas. Join one of the many electronic mailing lists available to PE professionals, including the chat section of www.pe4life.org, and the NASPE PE Talk board at www.lyris.sportime.com. After you get your feet wet, you'll be amazed at how one source leads to many others.

It Can Happen: A PE4life Success Story in Titusville, Pennsylvania

Before the 1998–99 school year, the health and physical education program in the Titusville (Pennsylvania) Area School District was like almost every program in the United States. The program was structured on athletics, and athletes dominated the classes. Teaching of sport skills was emphasized. Those who needed the benefit of exercise were either ignored or left in the wake of those more skilled.

Fortunately, our district administrators are very progressive in their thinking and were open to a change in the physical education department. It was at this time that we learned of the physical education program at Madison Junior High School in the Naperville (Illinois) Community Unit School District 203, and its leader, Phil Lawler. Our district allowed us to visit the

(continued)

Titusville, Pennsylvania *(continued)*

PE4life Academy at Madison and Naperville Central High School with the thought of "borrowing" ideas to enhance our program.

After attending the PE4life Academy, the groundwork for improvements in our program began with meetings and presentations to our school board and the local medical community. As with most school boards, money was an issue. However, the board was committed to spending monies if it was in the best interest of the education of our students. The medical community offered their expertise to support changes that would enable students to develop healthy habits. The first step in developing a PE4life Program was the development of a wellness center, complete with exercise equipment appropriate for all middle school students, including special needs students. Technology was also infused with the introduction of Polar heart rate monitors. This first year was spent concentrating on implementation of

PE4life philosophies and alignment of our curriculum to NASPE standards. Completion of a successful first year of change provided the impetus for further developments in the Titusville program.

At the middle school level we added a new class called wellness education, for our sixth-grade students. The high school has experienced the greatest degree of change—physical education is now offered to our students on a daily basis, worth one full credit, equal to all core subjects. Partnerships with numerous organizations have enhanced our delivery, and the media has played a crucial part in the development of our program.

Without the PE4life Academy, our schools would never have been inspired to make these dramatic changes to the way we approach physical education.

Tim McCord,
PE4life Academy director,
Titusville, Pennsylvania

Taking Action

Now that you've completed your PE4life Academy training, we encourage you to continue to develop your action plan to build a PE4life Program in your school or school district. Setting deadlines, communicating your efforts, and documenting your efforts will be key tasks in moving toward success. For each of the steps outlined in this manual, identify a target date for completing the tasks and begin documenting your actions and the results that they produce.

You can start by collecting the action plan worksheets in this manual and using them as the foundation for your customized action plan. Build

in regular checkpoints so that you can modify your plan if necessary and measure your progress toward becoming a state-of-the-art physical education program.

Developing and maintaining a passionate belief in the mission is the most important step toward effecting real change in your school and community. Beyond that, we strongly encourage you to use this book as a guiding tool (this process works!); tap into www.pe4life.org for loads of great resources and ideas; and exchange ideas, thoughts, and concerns with fellow PE4life Academy graduates and other like-minded colleagues in the field. New opportunities in the PE field are plentiful.

In dealing with physical education challenges and roadblocks, a key question to ask is, "What's important for the rest of students' lives?" Answer this question as part of your advocacy for PE and as an aid in building your PE4life program.

_____

_____

_____

How might you overcome the argument that there's not enough time in the school day to have daily PE?

_____

_____

_____

How might you overcome the mind-set of your "old school" PE colleagues?

_____

_____

_____

What are your PE technology tool priorities (e.g., heart monitors, pedometers, fitness software)?

_____

_____

_____

How can you enhance the perceived value of physical education in the minds of each of your key target audiences?

_____

_____

_____

What do you see as the three biggest potential roadblocks to implementing a PE4life program in your situation?

_____

_____

_____

What are your initial thoughts on dealing with these potential roadblocks?

_____

_____

_____

From _PE4life: Developing and Promoting Quality Physical Education,_ by PE4life, 2007, Champaign, IL: Human Kinetics.

How can your PE advisory group and other community allies help you address these potential roadblocks?

_____

_____

_____

Take the Next Steps

What are your priorities for the following time frames?

Next six months

_____

_____

_____

First year

_____

_____

_____

Step 7: Implementation Plan

Task	Who is responsible?	When will it be completed?

Document the Results

What results did you see at the following times?

Six months

_____

_____

_____

One year

_____

_____

_____

Two years

_____

_____

_____

From *PE4life: Developing and Promoting Quality Physical Education,* by PE4life, 2007, Champaign, IL: Human Kinetics.

IMPLEMENTING THE PE4life PROGRAM

CHAPTER 8

Turn Your Plan Into a Curriculum

Importance of Solid Curriculum Framework

In chapter 5 we provided an overview of the components of a PE4life Program along with examples of activities, program criteria, and curriculum development. In this chapter we take a more detailed look at curriculum development, which is an important step in putting your plan into action.

A well-written curriculum provides a structured, developmentally appropriate progression for teaching the concepts, skills, and attitudes that your students need to live active, fit, and healthy lives. This progression reinforces prerequisite skills and knowledge through their use and application, and continually introduces new concepts and skills to extend and challenge students, all while including regular and developmentally appropriate activity. Learning doesn't happen by accident, and an excellent curriculum is vital to student learning.

The curriculum is also an important advocacy tool because it communicates this information to teachers and other stakeholders, such as parents and administrators, who play a role in the success of your program. Gaining support for your program is much easier when you can articulate your goals and objectives, explain how you plan to reach them, and describe how you will know whether you have reached them (see chapter 10 for more information about assessment). If you don't have a well-written curriculum, administrators, parents, the school board, and others can easily dismiss physical education as a lesser component of the overall school program.

As mentioned in chapter 2, an important first step in developing your curriculum is to write a mission statement for your program and outline a basic framework. Here is an example of a mission statement and basic framework (NASPE, 2005c; Corbin & Lindsey, 2007; USDHHS, 2000).

Anytown Unified District Physical Education Program Mission Statement

The mission of the Anytown Unified School District Physical Education Program is to provide students, in a progressive and developmentally appropriate manner, the knowledge, skills, and attitudes necessary for living active, fit, and healthy lives. Ultimately it is our goal that our students are prepared to be productive members of society who take lifelong personal responsibility for engaging in health-related physical activity, not only because it's good for the body but also because they know how intrinsically rewarding it is to move in ways they enjoy.

Specifically, the Anytown Unified District Physical Education Program does the following:

- Provides planned, sequential physical education curricula for all grades that encourage enjoyable, lifelong physical activity. These curricula emphasize settings and activity parameters for lifetime activity.
- Integrates regular fitness testing into the curricula, but uses fitness test results for educational purposes, not report card grades. The fitness test used is Fitnessgram, which provides well-researched health-related fitness criteria.
- Is based on the state physical education content standards and the NASPE national content standards for physical education, designed to develop the physical, cognitive, and affective domains in children.
- Promotes enjoyable participation by using active learning strategies; developing students' knowledge, confidence, motor skills, and behavioral skills; and providing opportunities for regular physical activity.
- Promotes responsible personal and social behavior in physical activity settings.

Titusville Area School District: Health and Physical Education Department

The mission of the Titusville Area School District's physical education program is to encourage all students to sustain regular, lifelong physical activity as a foundation for a healthy, productive, and fulfilling life.

Senior High School Philosophy

The Titusville High School physical education program provides a progressive curriculum with a wide variety of experiences that challenges our students, builds on acquired skills, and imparts additional skills necessary to remain healthy and active throughout life.

Middle School Philosophy

The Titusville Middle School physical education program provides opportunities for all students, regardless of ability, to take part in activities in which they can achieve personal success, increase knowledge, improve skills and fitness, and learn the importance of teamwork, cooperation, effort, and sportsmanship.

Elementary Philosophy

The Titusville Elementary physical education program contributes to the social, emotional, mental, and physical well-being of children primarily through movement experiences. The development of basic motor skill competence, leadership skills, and fair play is emphasized as students engage in individual, cooperative, and competitive situations. Students learn a logical progression of skills through developmentally appropriate activities. Activities are structured for maximum participation and designed for individual success and safety regardless of the student's skill level.

Early Childhood Philosophy

The Titusville Early Childhood physical education program enhances cross-curricular learning through a multitude of sensory and movement activities based on cutting-edge brain research. Activities are structured for maximum participation and designed for individual success and safety regardless of the student's skill level.

Planning Progression

An important concept to keep in mind when developing your curriculum is that fitness and health cannot be stored and used later. Getting your students active on a regular basis is an important goal, and your students will enjoy the benefits of an active lifestyle while in school. After they graduate, however, they will be on their own. If they do not remain active on a regular basis as adults, the benefits that they gained from pursuing an active lifestyle in school will quickly disappear.

Therefore, you must design your curriculum so that your students assume progressively more responsibility for their own activity, fitness, and wellness. The Stairway to Lifetime Fitness, developed by Corbin and Lindsey (2007), provides an excellent outline of this approach (see figure 8.1). Another

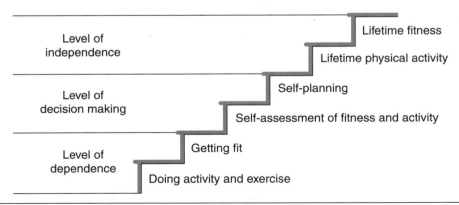

Figure 8.1 Students should assume progressively more responsibility for their own activity, fitness, and wellness, as illustrated by the Stairway to Lifetime Fitness.

Reprinted, by permission, from C.B. Corbin and R. Lindsey, 2007, *Fitness for life,* Updated 5th ed. (Champaign, IL: Human Kinetics), 14.

effective visual to help plan progression is provided by Kelly and Melograno (2004) (see figure 8.2).

A good method for planning progression is to design down and deliver up (Hopple, 2005 [see figure 8.3]; Kelly & Melograno, 2004; NASPE, 2005c). So, first determine your exit goal, which should be compatible with your mission statement. For example, the exit goal could be "When students graduate from Anytown High School, they will have the knowledge, skills, and appreciation needed to live active, fit, healthy lives on their own."

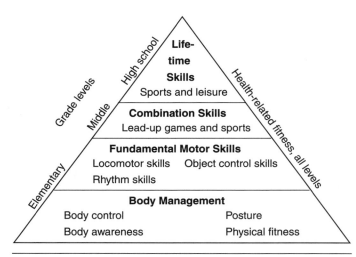

Figure 8.2 This pyramid illustrates the philosophy of building a progressive curriculum.

Reprinted, by permission, from L. Kelly and V. Melograno, 2004, *Developing the physical education curriculum: An achievement-based approach* (Champaign, IL: Human Kinetics), 70.

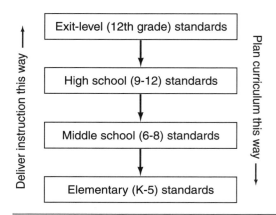

Figure 8.3 Designing-down and delivering up sequence.

Reprinted, by permission, from C.J. Hopple, 2005, *Elementary physical education teaching & assessment: A practical guide,* 2nd ed. (Champaign, IL: Human Kinetics), 60.

Next, you need to determine what you should teach in high school to achieve this exit goal. Following that, you need to determine what you should teach in middle school to prepare high school students to participate successfully in that program. Finally, you need to determine what basic skills and knowledge you should teach at the elementary level to provide a solid foundation for students who are entering middle school.

After you determine the scope and sequence of the curriculum, you must deliver the goods. Let's go over what an articulated K–12 physical education curriculum might look like in a PE4life Program.

Primary Level (K–Grade 2)

You start by building a solid foundation at the primary level. Teach children body control, body awareness, locomotor skills, rhythm skills, and object control (manipulative) skills, and give them plenty of time to practice. Students should start to understand that activity has an effect on the body (e.g., the heart beats faster and muscles get tired but stronger). You should expose students to fitness testing and practice the various tests, but you do not need to keep track of their scores yet. At this age level you can use loosely organized games to help children practice basic body control and various skills as they learn that activity can be fun. Any equipment used should be age appropriate. For example, when teaching throwing and catching, use soft, colorful, large balls to start. You might even use balloons at first. Rackets and bats should be an appropriate length and weight.

Following is a sample of what a K–2 curriculum might look like:

Primary Level Curriculum

Organization and rules for participating in physical education

Team building

Practice of Fitnessgram testing

Fitness activities and concepts

Identifying body parts

Running, personal space

Jumping, skipping, galloping

Throwing and catching

Kicking and striking

Rhythmic activities

Jump rope

Body shapes

Educational gymnastics

Loosely organized games or small-sided games

Manipulative games

Fitness concepts

Upper Elementary (Grades 3–5)

For successful participation in the middle school curriculum, students will need to have acquired some skills at the upper elementary level, including locomotor skills, object control (manipulative) skills, and rhythm skills. In addition, students should receive an introduction to sports through use of small-sided lead-up games and other sport-related activities that promote the use of skills and tactics in a developmentally appropriate manner. The skills theme approach advocated by Graham (2001) and Gallahue and Donnelly (2003) is an excellent approach.

Students should also begin learning the basics of health-related fitness and should be introduced to fitness testing, with an emphasis on using the tests for educational purposes. You can introduce fourth- and fifth-grade students to pedometers, heart rate monitors, and other technology and equipment.

Teach classes in a manner that emphasizes that activity can be fun and that students need to participate in a way that displays personal and social responsibility. Personal and social responsibility should be a lesson focus throughout the year. For ideas on how to do this, see resources listed in appendix C.

Following is what an upper-elementary curriculum might look like:

Third- and Fourth-Grade Curriculum

Team building

Fitness concepts or Fitnessgram testing (with focus on aerobic fitness)

Invasion games

Dance and rhythms

New or wall games

Educational gymnastics

Target games

Fitness concepts or Fitnessgram testing (with focus on muscular strength and endurance)

Striking or fielding games

Fitness concepts or Fitnessgram testing (with focus on flexibility and maybe introduce body composition)

Field days and special events

Fifth-Grade Curriculum

Team building

Fitness concepts or Fitnessgram testing (with focus on overall health-related fitness)

Soccer lead-up activities and games

Touch football lead-up games

Badminton lead-up games

Volleyball lead-up games

Basketball lead-up games

Aerobic fitness unit

Muscular strength and endurance and flexibility unit

Dance

Educational gymnastics

Softball lead-up games

Tennis lead-up games

Track and field events (developmentally appropriate approach)

Middle School (Grades 6–8)

Middle school is a vital transitional period. You need to help your students build on the basics that they learned in elementary school and prepare them to begin making choices in high school. Therefore, you should provide middle school students with a variety of physical activity experiences so that they can discover which activities they most enjoy (and would most likely continue to participate in as adults).

Students should also learn the skills and tactics necessary for successful participation in a variety of activities and sports. In particular, students should now be learning how to use skills and tactics in combination, in small-sided and some full-sided games.

Health-related fitness concepts and benefits should also be stressed as part of the curriculum at the middle school level. Students should now be gaining the knowledge that they will apply in the ninth-grade Fitness for Life course and in the electives that they will take in 10th through 12th grades.

At the middle school level, fitness testing should begin to move from teacher assessment to self-assessment. You should expose students to technology, such as pedometers, heart rate monitors, Fitnessgram and Activitygram software, the Tri-Fit machine, Microfit, fitness equipment, and so on.

You should emphasize that physical activity can be enjoyable and social. Research has consistently shown that the middle school level is a time when many previously active children become more sedentary. We don't want to lose them to computer games, television, and hanging out at the mall. Therefore, expose students to the benefits of activity, which at this age includes having fun with friends, feeling and looking good, and being more independent. Although teaching long-term health benefits is important, those benefits tend to be less meaningful to middle school students.

In addition, you should teach personal and social responsibility in physical activity settings to prepare students for appropriate participation in high school. An excellent approach is to offer a unit on team building at the start of each year in middle school (Midura &

Glover, 2005) and then reinforce the learning throughout each year (Hellison, 2003; Glover & Anderson, 2003). See appendix C for sample team-building activities.

A middle school curriculum might look something like the following, although the selection of specific sports and activities will need to be based on local facilities, equipment, teacher expertise, scheduling, and other factors.

Sixth-Grade Curriculum

Team building

Fitnessgram testing (pretesting)

Touch football

Soccer

Fitness walking and jogging

Volleyball

Strength and conditioning (weight training and flexibility)

Basketball

Dance

Educational gymnastics

Badminton

Bowling

Aerobic conditioning

Fitnessgram testing (posttesting)

Softball

Track and field events

Swimming

Seventh-Grade Curriculum

Team building

Fitness concepts (with focus on technology)

Fitnessgram testing (pretesting)

Flag football or soccer (advanced)

Fitness walking, jogging, or running (advanced)

Strength and conditioning (weight training and flexibility)

Basketball (advanced)

Dance

Tumbling

Floor hockey

Table tennis

Aerobic conditioning

Fitnessgram testing (posttesting)

Softball (advanced)

Tennis

Golf

Eighth-Grade Curriculum

Team building

Fitnessgram testing (pretesting self-assessment)

Fitness concepts (program planning)

Team sports (select one: touch football, soccer, or Ultimate)

Individual activity (select one: walking, jogging, or running; cycling; or wall climbing)

Team sports (select one: basketball, volleyball, or floor hockey)

Strength and conditioning (weight training and flexibility)

Individual or dual sports (select one: badminton, table tennis, gymnastics, bowling, or dance)

Aerobic conditioning

Fitnessgram testing (posttesting self-assessment)

Team or individual dual sports (select one: softball, tennis, swimming, track and field, or golf)

Phil Lawler on Team Building

Team building is good for your students, and once teachers are trained in adventure education, it will change the way that they teach. It will change the way that they view students and dramatically improve their relationships with students.

Here is something that schools might want to try to get students more engaged. At the start of each quarter you can assign or ask students to pick class responsibilities. Examples include the following:

- Medical helpers. If a student has a minor injury but needs to go to the nurse, the "MX" students assist the student to the nurse. Once these students select this duty, they go to the nurse, introduce themselves, and tell the nurse about their new responsibility.

- Time management students. Students are allowed to be clock watchers. If a teacher is giving an introductory lesson and does not want to spend too much time, the students let the teacher know when the time limit is up. This helps to keep the teacher on task. It helps when we try to have 80 percent of each class period with students active. Lectures are important,

but sometimes teachers lose track of time when they don't have a helper.

- Welcome wagon. When a new student moves into the school, these students help the new student make the adjustments. Another important task for the welcome wagon: Any time there is a substitute teacher, the students welcome the teacher and answer any questions that the teacher might have about class procedures.

- Student news reporters. These students tell the teacher any good news about students in the class, such as an award that a student received outside of school. The teacher can then announce it to the class. News may just be to note a student's birthday, which the teacher can announce to the class. Announcing students' success in front of their peers is a great way to make students feel important.

- Equipment crew. These students help the teacher set up equipment before class or break it down after class. This group is particularly important for the first hour and last hour of the day.

(continued)

Team Building   *(continued)*

- Class clown. Selection and guidelines are important, but a class clown can keep us from taking ourselves too seriously. This student is allowed to stop the class and share a joke or a funny story when things are dragging.
- Errand runner. This role is for trustworthy students. These students can run special errands during class, such as to retrieve something that the teacher forgot in her or his office.

Teachers can create other types of student helpers. They can rotate the workers each quarter or semester so that every student performs a job during the year.

High School (Grades 9–12)

If we expect our students to become independent consumers of physical activity as adults, we must provide them with the appropriate tools and experiences. They need skills for self-management and program planning. They must learn how to overcome barriers, how to be effective consumers, and how to be safe. And we must provide them time to practice these skills. Here is one way in which you might organize a high school program to accomplish these goals:

- **9th grade**. All students take a one-semester Fitness for Life course (Corbin & Lindsey, 2007) in which they develop the foundational skills and knowledge necessary for living a physically active and healthy life. This course combines lectures with activities and focuses on independent decision making. Technology helps students learn to self-assess their fitness, activity levels, and nutrition, and create personal fitness, activity, and nutrition plans based on where they are now and where they want to go. In addition, an online study guide available with the book *Fitness for Life* provides more flexibility in offering this course.

This course also helps students take a good look at themselves in terms of the type of activities that they most enjoy, and thus are most likely to continue as adults. For example, students complete self-evaluations to determine whether they most enjoy competition or cooperation, whether they like team sports and social settings or individual sports and solo activities, whether they like being outdoors or indoors, and so on.

During the other semester all students take a freshman orientation physical education course in which they have the opportunity to explore a variety of lifelong activities, with emphasis on activities available in the local community.

- **10th to 12th grades**. Students pick electives based on what they learned in the Fitness for Life course and the experiences that they had with various activities in the freshman orientation course.

The electives are one-semester courses that are grouped by interest and skill level, rather than by grade level, so that more variety can be provided. These courses prepare students for their chosen activities more thoroughly than did the units that they took in previous years. Discussion of the health benefits of the activities occurs as the students are learning and practicing skills.

An important element of these courses is teaching students how to continue the activity as adults. Besides the classroom element, the courses include field trips to facilities in the community so that students can make the connection between what they are learning in class and the opportunities available to continue the activity as adults. Guest teachers from the community come in to share their expertise and reinforce the connection between classroom instruction and community opportunities. Here are a few ideas for guest teachers, instructors, or speakers:

- Director of adult sports from the local parks and recreation department, to talk about how teams are formed and how adult sports leagues operate

- Representatives from local cycling, running, or dance clubs, to talk about club activities and how to join
- Local tennis or golf pro, to talk about leagues, tournaments, and lessons available for adults
- Owner of a health and fitness club, to talk about membership, equipment, and classes that are available
- Owner of a bowling alley, to talk about leagues, open bowling, and tournaments
- A local martial arts expert, to talk about classes and competition
- Representatives from other area recreational facilities, such as a wall-climbing facility, ski hill, canoe rental business, in-line skating and

adventure sports store, to speak about the activities that they support

These local experts can provide instructional tips. In addition, they can show students what to look for when buying any needed equipment, including quality, pricing, and where to buy it.

The elective courses that you offer will depend on the expertise of your teaching staff, available facilities and equipment, and what is available in your community. An excellent example of a well-thought-out offering of electives is provided in the box below by Paul Zientarski, department chair, Naperville (Illinois) Central High School (Paul explains his program on the DVD included with this book). Another example is from Lake Park High School in Roselle, Illinois (see figure 8.4).

These examples of activities across grade levels give you a starting point in thinking about the scope and sequence of your curriculum. Much will depend on your local environment. For example, in some places activities like skiing, snowshoeing, and orienteering might be good choices, whereas in other areas swimming, canoeing, hiking, and mountain biking may be more feasible. Schools in an urban environment might emphasize fitness walking, using fitness clubs, and playing sports offered by the parks and recreation department.

Naperville Central High School Physical Education Activities

Activities from this list are offered on a selected basis as determined by the department. All upper class members select activities from the various groups to ensure that they receive a broad-based exposure to the various types of activities. Students are required to pass six fitness classes, four team sports, three individual sports, two aquatics, two gymnastics, two dance, and CPR.

Freshmen are enrolled in a core group of activities, which includes soccer, flag football, gymnastics, square dance, volleyball, basic swimming, wrestling, badminton, and fitness orientation.

(continued)

Individual sports	Team sports	Physical fitness activities
Archery	Basketball	Aerobics
Badminton	Flag football	Circuit training
Basic gymnastics	Floor hockey	Cross-training
Basic wrestling	Indoor soccer	Frosh fitness orientation
Cross-country skiing	Passball	Jogging and conditioning
Golf	Soccer	Kickboxing
Gymnastics and tumbling	Softball	Step aerobics
In-line skating	Team handball	Weight training
Racquetball	Volleyball	
Tennis	Four-sport indoor and outdoor	
Rhythmic activities	**Aquatics**	**Others**
Advanced dance, social and square	Aquanastics	Adapted PE
Basic dance	Basic swimming	CPR certification
Line dance	Life guard certification	First-aid certification
Social dance	Swim fitness	High-ropes course
Square dance	Water games	Rock climbing
Swing dance		Team building
Tap dance		

Physical Education Department Course Offerings

9th grade		10th grade	
Physical education 1st or 2nd semester	Health education 1st or 2nd semester	Physical education 1st or 2nd semester	Driver education 1st or 2nd semester
Restrictive physical education 1st and 2nd semesters		Restrictive physical education 1st and 2nd semesters	

11th and 12th grades		
Introduction to dance arts	Strength and conditioning 1st and 2nd semesters	Strength training
Team activities 1st and 2nd semesters	Cross-training Aerobic wellness	Continuing dance arts
Personal wellness: Nutrition and exercise		Off-campus individual activities 1st and 2nd semesters
Restrictive physical education 1st and 2nd semesters		Leadership training Fitness certification
		Leadership training Coaching certification
		Restrictive physical education 1st and 2nd semesters

Figure 8.4   An excellent example of course offerings from Lake Park High School in Roselle, Illinois.
Reprinted by permission of Debra Vogel.

Curriculum Models

PE4life provides criteria for a quality physical education program, but it does not advocate a specific curriculum to meet these criteria.

Several commonly used curriculum models in physical education can successfully meet the PE4life criteria. These include fitness education, sport education, personal responsibility, activities and sports, movement education, skill themes, adventure education, interdisciplinary, and student centered. See appendix E for resources that provide detailed information on these curriculum models.

The approach that we've used as an example in this chapter is an eclectic one that combines several curriculum models with a focus on lifetime physical activity and fitness. This is the approach advocated by the Physical Best program (NASPE, 2005c), which is not a complete curriculum but rather a fitness education program used to enhance a complete curriculum. The Physical Best program provides comprehensive information but gives local administrators and teachers a great deal of flexibility.

Complete curriculums that are more prescriptive are also available. An example is the SPARK program. Information about the SPARK program is available at www.sparkpe.org.

You can achieve the goals of a quality physical education program through a variety of curriculum models, but whatever model you select, the curriculum must be in writing, provide a developmentally appropriate progression, include built-in assessment (see chapter 10), and be consistent with national and state standards and your local mission statement and objectives.

CHAPTER 9

Implement Your Curriculum

Teaching Effectively

In this chapter we show you how to bring life to your curriculum by implementing appropriate teaching strategies, selecting excellent learning activities, and incorporating PE4life principles.

An outstanding curriculum does little good if it is not delivered through effective teaching. Gallahue and Donnelly (2003) defined effective teachers as those who, through planned instruction, are able to bring about positive changes in learning. Such changes occur in a meaningful, nonthreatening environment that helps to develop a thinking and acting person.

Personal Traits

Gallahue and Donnelly (2003) offered a detailed list of personal traits that you must possess to be an effective teacher:

- **Show interest in your students**. Display an interest in students as individuals, while not being friendly to the point that you cannot act as a disciplinarian if necessary. Try to provide positive and specific feedback, speak personally to students and call them by name, give students responsibilities, deal with students equitably, and build students' self-esteem (remember birthdays, likes and dislikes, and so on).

> Perhaps the most important thing to remember about effective teaching can be summarized in this old adage: "Students don't care how much you know until they know how much you care."

- **Be honest.** Don't be condescending, and be willing to admit mistakes.

- **Be enthusiastic.** Be upbeat in your teaching. If you're not enthusiastic about the subject, your students won't be either.

- **Show that you are human.** Simple things like a smile and showing a sense of humor can show your students that you are human.

- **Be courteous.** Respect students as worthwhile human beings and insist that they respect each other. Use positive terms like "please" and "thank you." Model the behavior that you want to see.

- **Speak effectively.** Use a clear voice and vocabulary geared to your students' level, but do not talk down to your students.

- **Be confident.** Be a leader, but do not enhance your ego at your students' expense.

- **Dress properly.** Personal appearance affects how students view you. Dress professionally and appropriately for the lessons that you are teaching on a given day. You are a teacher, not a recreation leader.

- **Be knowledgeable.** Stay up to date with your profession. The resources listed in appendixes B and E offer many ways to help you stay current. An excellent teaching strategy is to share new knowledge with your students. For example, if you read a new study in a journal that showed that most *Fortune* 500 CEOs live active lifestyles, share that information with your students. Doing so will show that you are keeping up to date and will provide more evi-

dence of the relevance of physical education to their lives.

Conduct in the Classroom

Effective teachers must remember that many aspects of their classroom conduct will influence their students' success. Think about several things that you can do to become more effective:

- **Maximize participation.** Strive to keep management time at or below 15 percent so that at least 85 percent of class time is available for active participation.

- **Teach by objective.** Have clearly stated objectives for each lesson and communicate these to your students when you introduce the lesson.

- **Arrive promptly.** Model the behavior that you want to see.

- **Prepare.** A well-prepared class goes by quickly because time is allocated and used wisely.

- **Use resources.** When appropriate, use outside resources. For example, when teaching a strength-training unit, bring in a certified personal trainer to talk to your students. Or when teaching a dance unit, bring in a dance instructor from the community to give a demonstration.

- **Review and preview.** Provide a brief verbal or visual review of the previous lesson and a preview of the material that you will cover in the current lesson. This procedure allows students to link previous information with new information and follow the day's lesson more closely.

- **Check for understanding.** Do not assume that students automatically understand instruction; constantly check for understanding by asking strategic questions. For example, ask your students whether the ability to do 50 push-ups is a sign of good muscular strength or a sign of good muscular endurance. Their answer will let you know whether they comprehend the concept.

- **Stress practicality.** Emphasize practical application of the material that you teach so that students can

accurately and personally apply the information in their own lives. For example, when introducing a volleyball unit, talk about the local adult co-ed volleyball league offered by the local parks and recreation department and how people can enjoy the sport for both fitness and fun for a lifetime.

- **Think realistically.** Be realistic about how much material students can learn in the time available. It's better for students to learn a few things well rather than many things inadequately.

- **Remain open.** Be open to student questions and comments and create a forum for exchange of ideas. This process encourages students to think and synthesize information.

- **Speak clearly.** Clearly state objectives in language that students understand. Do not overload students with verbiage.

- **Stay in control.** Be objective, consistent, and constructive in applying disciplinary measures.

Assessment

Assessment allows teachers to see students' progress within the program. To maximize effective assessment, do the following:

- **Assess by objectives.** Set objectives for your lessons and then provide assessment to determine if those objectives were achieved.

- **Use valid instruments.** Each assessment should be based on a test that is valid and relevant to the objective being assessed.

- **Vary techniques.** Use a variety of assessments to ensure a total picture of your students' progress. For example, to measure students' knowledge of weight-training techniques, you might first give a multiple-choice quiz. You could then observe students as they perform the techniques to see whether they use the correct form. Later you could have students teach the technique to other students, using a checklist to measure how many key components they teach.

- **Respond in a timely manner.** Provide meaningful feedback to students as quickly as possible. This method helps students focus on strengths and weaknesses and ensures that the assessment process is truly part of the learning process.

- **Show understanding.** Realize that students perceive things differently. If you exhibit understanding, your students will know that you are interested enough in them to listen to their interpretations and the reasons for their answers.

- **Stay informed.** Recognize that external factors may affect student performance. Take time to learn about your students as individuals and find out what they do outside school.

- **Treat students fairly.** Do not let personal prejudice, bias, or preference interfere with fair and honest assessment. Evaluate students on what they know and can do, not on style of dress or likeability.

If with reasonable effort students can attain the tasks that teachers present, then students will likely be more encouraged to achieve the tasks. Thus, the logical next step to becoming an effective teacher is to consider how to design and plan to help students achieve program goals.

While planning and designing physical education, teachers must consider the type of teaching style that they will use. The teaching style is the manner in which the planned program will effectively reach the students.

Implications for Practice

1. Design practice so that students are engaged at a high level and are successful with effort for sufficient time to produce learning.

2. Design practice conditions to be as gamelike as students can cope with successfully.

3. Design curriculum so that students develop skills through careful articulation of progressions over the grade levels.

4. Design tasks so that the learner can achieve them with effort.

5. Plan progressions that go from simple to complex and have available many ways to practice skills at the same level.

6. Manipulate the demands of motor tasks by manipulating the context (conditions of practice) of the task for individual learners.

7. Develop good management skills so that you can teach using a variety of effective teaching methods.

8. When the objective is to give the learner a clear idea of how to perform a motor task, use a combination of verbal and visual information and verbal rehearsal.

9. Design learning cues for skills that accurately and richly reflect the required movement characteristics.

10. Use specific feedback to provide information to learners and to motivate and keep practice focused in large-group instruction.

11. Understand the critical role of success and the perceived confidence of individual students and work with students to help them want to achieve the task for internal rather than imposed reasons.

Reprinted, by permission, from S. Silverman and C. Ennis, 2003, *Student learning in physical education*, 2nd ed. (Champaign, IL: Human Kinetics), 183.

Teaching Styles

Using a variety of teaching styles will help you improve student interest, enjoyment, and attitude toward physical activity (NASPE, 2005c). A spectrum of teaching styles, defined by Mosston and Ashworth (2002), moves along a continuum from direct instruction (teacher initiated) to indirect instruction (student initiated). The spectrum approach is an effective teaching strategy in helping your students assume progressively more responsibility for their own activity, fitness, and wellness, as illustrated in the Stairway to Lifetime Fitness (Corbin & Lindsey, 2007), outlined in the previous chapter.

• **Command.** The teacher makes all the decisions and gives step-by-step instructions. This style is used to introduce new skills, to teach specific tasks that involve safety issues (e.g., teaching CPR), and to work with classes that need structure.

• **Practice.** The teacher decides what to teach, introduces the skills, directs the time to be spent on the task, and circulates

among the students, giving feedback. The students decide the number of practice trials and the order in which they practice the skills. For example, you might ask high school students to take their heart rates into their target heart rate zones but allow them to choose from a number of different activities to do so.

- **Reciprocal.** The teacher designs the tasks to be performed, and students work collaboratively (usually in pairs or small groups), providing feedback to each other. This style begins to lead students to more independent, critical thinking. For example, in preparing for taking the Fitnessgram test, the teacher supplies students with checklists on proper test protocols, and students break into pairs and give each other feedback on technique.

- **Self-check.** This style is similar to the reciprocal style, but instead of working with others, students evaluate their own performance. The teacher still determines the tasks to be completed and designs the task or criteria sheet to be used. Then each student performs the tasks and provides his or her own feedback by completing the sheet. This style is best for refining skills and building self-reliance, because limited interaction occurs with the teacher and fellow students. This style works well for homework. For example, you might ask students to log aerobic fitness activity time performed outside class. Allow students to select the appropriate activities for themselves and to monitor their own progress, giving themselves feedback through self-assessment of their aerobic fitness.

- **Inclusion.** The teacher still designs the tasks to be completed, but students choose the difficulty level at which they want to perform. This approach puts the responsibility of learning back on the students because they decide when to move to a more difficult level of performance. Thus the teacher can empower students to move closer to independence. For example, when working on upper-body muscular strength and endurance, allow students to do modified push-ups, regular push-ups, or the bench press. Make sure that students know that they should increase the difficulty when they judge themselves ready to do so.

- **Guided discovery.** The teacher determines the task and then designs a sequence of questions or problems that will lead students to one right answer. An example of a guided discovery lesson is to assign students to write a report that answers the following questions:

  - What is one jogging or in-line skating route that allows you to jog or skate for 20 minutes starting from school or home (students might have to try several routes before they find one that meets the criteria)?
  - What safety issues do you need to pay attention to on the route that you select? Do these issues change with the time of day or weather?

- **Convergent discovery.** The teacher poses a problem or question and students go through the discovery process to converge on the one right answer without the teacher's guidance (while adhering to the principles of safety). For example, you could ask high school students to complete a report on what it would take to begin participating in a beneficial aerobic fitness activity in their community. Have them research the aerobic fitness benefits of various activities, find one that they can do in the community, find out the costs for equipment, learn where to do the activity, discover what prerequisite skills are necessary, and so on.

- **Divergent production.** The teacher poses an open-ended problem for students to solve—one that might have several correct answers. For example, in working with younger students, you might have them come up with three locomotor skills that will increase their heart rate.

- **Individual program—learner's design.** The teacher chooses the general subject area, but the student determines the task and possible solutions. For example, students could design their own personal health-related fitness plans.

(continued)

Teaching Styles (continued)

- **Learner initiated.** Students choose the general subject area and how they will go about completing the task on their own. This style, similar to contract learning, might be used with older students who have specific fitness or sport interests. Examples include having students prepare for elite competition in power lifting, figure skating, gymnastics, or other activities. Teacher direction would be present, but instruction and practice would take place outside class.

- **Self-teaching.** Students make virtually all the learning decisions. This method is appropriate with high school students who have proved that they can pursue learning independent of a teacher's direction.

Adapted, by permission, from National Association for Sport and Physical Education (NASPE), 2005, *Physical education for lifelong fitness: The Physical Best teacher's guide*, 2nd ed. (Champaign, IL: Human Kinetics), 160-161.

Selecting Appropriate Activities

The activity brings together everything that teachers have been planning to help their students achieve program goals, so activity selection is possibly the most important part of implementing the curriculum. The Activity Selection Criteria Checklist provides sample questions for teachers to consider as they select their activities.

Activity Selection Criteria Checklist

Look over all the components for selecting appropriate activities for your students.

- ___ Does the activity meet the needs of your student population (age and skill level, gender, special needs, and so forth)?

- ___ Do the objectives for the activity connect with your program goals and expected outcomes? NASPE outcomes? State standards?

- ___ Do you have the necessary facility and equipment?

- ___ Is the activity developmentally appropriate for your students (including complexity of instructions and skills required)?

- ___ Does this activity support maximum student participation, or can it be modified for greater or lesser student participation? (Use the 80/80 rule: A minimum of 80 percent of your students should be engaged in the activity a minimum of 80 percent of the time.)

- ___ Does the activity allow for a variety of difficulty levels (can it be modified for a younger or less skilled student and an older or more skilled student)?

- ___ Can the activity be applied in a setting other than a formal instructional setting?

- ___ Will the activity hold the interest of your students, or is boredom likely to set in?

- ___ Is the activity safe?

Reprinted, by permission, from National Association for Sport and Physical Education (NASPE), 2005, *Physical education for lifelong fitness: The Physical Best teacher's guide*, 2nd ed. (Champaign, IL: Human Kinetics), 155.

If a program is to prepare students to be independently active and healthy for a lifetime, activity selection is critical. The activities that you select should enhance your students' chances of reaching this ultimate goal. Key factors in activity selection (NASPE, 2005c) include the following:

• **Sequential.** Activities should progress in age-appropriate ways. The key is to build on the topic over the years so that students progress toward their goals (see table 9.1).

• **Enjoyable.** Learning is the goal, but enjoyment enhances the learning process and increases the chances that students will continue to be active as adults. Keep in mind that different students find different activities enjoyable.

• **Variety.** People can be active and healthy in many different ways. Offer variety and choices. For example, design a high school program with electives (see chapter 8). The body doesn't care whether it gets in shape through

Table 9.1 Sample Activity Progressions by Topic

	Primary (K–2)	Intermediate (3–5)	Middle school (6–8)	High school (9–12)
Corbin and Lindsey's Stairway to Lifetime Fitness (2007)	Step 1—doing regular exercise	Step 2—achieving physical fitness	Step 3—personal exercise patterns	Step 4—self-evaluation Step 5—problem solving and decision making
Heart rate	Place hand on heart before and after vigorous activity and compare HR	Count pulse; learn math to find HR based on partial count	Practice math to find HR based on partial count; graph HR monitor data; assess effort based on graphed data	Design workouts based on knowledge of HR and target HR zone
Running	Learn correct stride; run in low-organization games	Analyze running strides of peers using rubric; design low-organization games that incorporate a large amount of running	Teach peers to run more efficiently; report on how running efficiently helps a person succeed in a favorite sport	Design interval workouts that alternate high- and low-intensity effort as determined by HR; make the workout fun for a friend to do
Upper-body strength training	Play on the monkey bars on the playground	Play fun push-up games (see Hichwa, 1998); learn tubing exercises	Learn more tubing exercises; design games that increase muscular strength without equipment	Learn how to lift weights safely; design a personal weight-training program; explore community options for weight training and do cost analysis
Throwing and catching	Learn basic skills; apply in low-organization, small-sided games	Design low-organization, small-sided games to practice the skills; self-analyze what makes a throw stronger	Modify a physical activity that involves these skills to include a stronger aerobic fitness component	Apply skill in more complex games; analyze similarities in the use of the skills among several sports

Reprinted, by permission, from National Association for Sport and Physical Education (NASPE), 2005, *Physical education for lifelong fitness: The Physical Best teacher's guide,* 2nd ed. (Champaign, IL: Human Kinetics), 153.

basketball, dancing, kayaking, cross-country skiing, or swimming. Offering students a chance to select activities can increase participation and decrease discipline problems.

- **Active participation by everyone.** Each student should be an active participant in the activities that you select. Use the following ideas to ensure participation (NASPE, 2005c):

  - Supply enough equipment (e.g., one ball per child).

  - Set up small-sided games so that turns are more frequent.

  - Run several games at once so that an eliminated player rotates to another group and continues to play.

  - Modify rules to keep everyone playing (e.g., in a tag game have helpers who unfreeze taggers quickly). See the cup-stacking lesson in appendix C, contributed by Rick Schupbach, as an example of modifying rules to keep all students active.

  - Have baseball batting teams perform locomotor tasks while the base runner runs the bases so that all students are active.

- **Connected.** Connect activities to real life whenever possible, an element emphasized by the Physical Best program. For example, you should let elementary students know that playing small-sided soccer games now will prepare them to play real soccer when they are older. Help older students see the connections between being physically active and looking and feeling better. As students move from middle school to high school, you should select activities that are relevant to them both in school and in their future. Show them what is available in their community to help them be active as young adults. Are there bike paths, adult sport leagues, swimming pools that offer adult lap swimming, health and fitness clubs, running clubs, dance clubs, kayaking outfitters, or other opportunities? Take field trips to these places. Invite community activity leaders to your school to offer demonstrations to your students and talk about opportunities for adults. Assign homework that relates in-school activity to the adult world. For example, have students write a paper about which fitness club or sport league they would join based on their personal interests. Another idea is to have them determine the costs of taking up an activity. For example, for skiing, they would learn about the cost of equipment, lift tickets (if downhill), transportation, and so on.

Another example is the Bounce at the Bell lesson plan, which is directly connected to research on healthy bone growth. This is described in the lesson plan example found in appendix C.

- **Individualized.** Individualize each lesson as much as possible to ensure developmental appropriateness and, therefore, success and benefits for each student. You may have to adjust the difficulty of tasks for an individual or small group. An excellent example of this is the slanty rope theory, proposed by Mosston and Ashworth (1986). The theory suggests that, given options, children will choose the one that offers the maximum challenge but also allows them to be successful. The classic example is to put two ropes on the floor in a V shape and have students practice jumping from one side to another, self-selecting at which point (narrow, wide, or in between) they wish to jump. Skilled students can challenge themselves at the wide point, and those with less skill can have success at the narrow point and work their way up. An example for high school students might be an assignment to design and implement their own fitness plan to meet a specific goal. Some students might have a goal of losing a modest amount of weight or being able to run a mile continuously without having to stop and rest, whereas other students might have a goal of running a local 10K road race and finishing in the top 10 of all runners.

Importance of Teaching Goal Setting and Self-Management

It is very important that you teach your students goal setting and self-management so that they will become responsible for their own activity, fitness, and health for a lifetime. Thus, you must create lessons and select activities that help your students learn these important skills. An excellent discussion about how to do this appears on pages 28 through 34 in *Physical Education for Lifelong Fitness: The Physical Best Teacher's Guide* (NASPE, 2005c). In addition, goal setting and self-management is emphasized in the Fitness for Life curriculum (see www.fitnessforlife.org for more information).

Inclusion

The Physical Best program defines inclusion as the process of creating a learning environment that is open to and effective for all students whose needs and abilities fall outside the general range of those for children of similar age or whose cultural or religious beliefs differ from that of the majority group. In short, inclusion means that all students are included in a way that all can reach their maximum potential. To learn more about appropriate inclusion strategies, read pages 179 through 198 of *Physical Education for Lifelong Fitness: The Physical Best Teacher's Guide* (NASPE, 2005c). Additional resources about inclusion can be found in appendix E.

Lesson Examples

The following examples will help you envision how your program planning, designing, and activity selection can become a reality in your classroom.

Physical Best Examples

The Physical Best program is an excellent example of using activities that support the goals and objectives of your lessons. We have included four examples in appendix C:

> At Least 10 Alligators (a lesson plan at the primary level)
> Sport Roundup (a lesson plan at the intermediate level)
> Fitting in Fitness (a lesson plan at the middle school level)
> Evaluating Health Products (a lesson plan at the middle and high school levels)

Additional resources for activities and lessons can be found in appendix E.

Team-Building Examples

Team building is the strategy of facilitating the development of a team through a series of purposeful activities and then assigning the team carefully constructed physical challenges to overcome. The people on the team must work together to develop and implement a strategy for achieving their objective (Midura & Glover, 2005). Many physical education teachers have found that a team-building unit is an excellent way to start a new school year.

Two examples of team-building lessons can be found in appendix C. Both of these examples, Bridge Over the Raging River and Indiana's Challenge, are intermediate challenges.

CHAPTER 10

Assess Your Students

Importance of Assessment

In chapter 6 we emphasized the need to develop a quality assessment plan, which really serves as a lifestyle prescription plan for each of your students. With this approach, students don't compete against each other, but instead measure their personal success based on daily, weekly, and yearly progress. In this chapter we provide more assessment details and examples.

To assess students and provide them helpful feedback, you should monitor progress in all learning domains (NASPE, 2005c): health-related fitness, psychomotor, affective, and cognitive.

The health-related fitness domain is most often assessed through fitness testing such as Fitnessgram. The psychomotor domain refers to skills and motor or movement patterns. Drills, skills tests, and gamelike activities are the common assessment tools. The affective domain refers to the attitudes and values that a student has toward and during physical activity. Although difficult to measure, affective behaviors can be assessed through journals, questionnaires, and systematic observation of student behaviors, including effort and compliance with directions. To increase the objectivity of affective assessment, create rubrics for tests and assignments that make it clear how behavior will be assessed. The cognitive domain refers to knowledge about rules, procedures, safety, and critical elements as well as fitness knowledge that will contribute to the ability to make healthy lifetime activity choices and participate in a variety of physical activities throughout life.

Health-Related Fitness Domain

Fitnessgram—which is valid and reliable, uses criterion-referenced standards associated with good health, and provides students with individualized feedback—is the recommended tool for the health-related fitness domain. Complete information on Fitnessgram can be found at www.fitnessgram.net. Once on the site, you can click on Reference Guide for detailed information about the science behind the creation of this test battery. The following introduction to Fitnessgram, adapted with permission from the Cooper Institute, appears in the online reference guide:

Fitnessgram is the national fitness test battery for youth. The Cooper Institute developed this assessment in response to the needs in physical education programs for a comprehensive assessment protocol. The assessment includes a variety of health-related physical fitness tests designed to assess cardiovascular fitness, muscle strength, muscular endurance, flexibility, and body composition. Criterion-referenced standards associated with good health have been established for children and youth for each of the health-related fitness components. The software for the program produces an individualized report card that summarizes the child's performance on each component of health-related fitness and provides suggestions for how to promote and maintain good fitness. The sophisticated database structure within the program produces compiled class reports and allows long-term tracking of the student's fitness over time.

Fitnessgram can be used by students to help them in personal fitness program planning, by teachers to determine student needs and to help guide students in program planning, and by parents to understand their child's needs and to help the child plan a program of physical activity. Additional information on the assessments of aerobic capacity, musculoskeletal fitness, and body composition is provided in other chapters [of the online reference guide]. Details about interpreting Fitnessgram reports can be found in the section on interpreting reports [in the online reference guide]. To read more, go to www.fitnessgram.net and click on Reference Guide.

Activitygram

Activitygram is a module within the Fitnessgram software that helps children and adolescents self-monitor their personal activity patterns. It provides a report for students, teachers, and parents as well as record-keeping functions for individuals and groups. Activitygram is designed to help students monitor their activity patterns and to plan personal activity programs for a lifetime. Activitygram uses the physical activity pyramid as a basis for analyzing personal activity patterns. Specific information on the Activitygram assessment is provided in the section on physical activity assessment. Details on interpreting Activitygram reports can be found in the section on interpreting reports, all in the online reference guide.

The acronym HELP describes the philosophy of Fitnessgram and Activitygram.

H = Health and health-related fitness

The primary goal of both programs is to promote regular physical activity among all youth. Of particular importance is promoting activity patterns that lead to reduced health risk and improved health-related physical fitness.

E = Everyone

Fitnessgram and Activitygram are designed for all people regardless of physical ability. They are intended to help all youth find some form of activity that they can do for a lifetime. Too often, activity programs are perceived to be only for those who are skilled or athletic rather than for all people.

L = Lifetime

Fitnessgram and Activitygram have as an immediate goal helping young people to be active now, but the long-term goal is to help them learn to do activities that they will continue to perform throughout their life.

P = Personal

No two people are the same. No two people enjoy all the same activities. Fitnessgram and Activitygram are designed to personalize physical activity to meet personal or individual needs.

Fitnessgram

Consistent with the Fitnessgram philosophy, the individual fitness tests and the full Fitnessgram test battery are designed to be used in several ways. The battery can be used for personal fitness self-testing (the primary use), personal best testing, institutional testing, parental reporting, and personal tracking.

• **Personal fitness self-testing.** Personal fitness self-testing is the principal use for Fitnessgram test items. Students are taught to give the tests to themselves and to interpret their test results. If this objective is met, students can test themselves and plan personal programs throughout life. Learning to self-test effectively takes a considerable amount of practice, so multiple opportunities to practice are

necessary. Self-testing results are considered to be personal. For this reason student information may be kept personal if a student desires. Personal Fitnessgram reports may be printed, but students decide whether they want to share their personal information. Students who fail to reach the healthy fitness zone will be assisted in developing a program of improvement. Students who reach the healthy fitness zone will be taught how to determine goals for fitness within the zone and how to maintain that level of fitness. Because students do their own testing, special teams of fitness testers are not necessary. Test results for beginning self-testers are not particularly accurate, and this point should be emphasized to students.

• **Personal best testing.** Personal best testing is for students who want to see how well they can perform on each fitness test item. Because such testing takes considerable time and because all children and youth may not be interested in this type of testing, personal best testing should be done before or after school on a voluntary basis. The Fitnessgram philosophy focuses on good health; extremely high levels of fitness are not necessary for good health. Some youth, however, may be interested in achieving high levels of fitness to achieve performance goals, so teachers may wish to provide the opportunity for such personal best testing.

• **Institutional testing.** Institutional testing helps teachers determine the fitness level of groups of students and may provide direction for curriculum planning. This type of testing requires teams of people trained in testing and takes a considerable amount of class time. The Fitnessgram advisers suggest that this type of testing be done only periodically, perhaps every third year. Pre- and posttesting (at the beginning of school and at the end of school) are not recommended because they take too much time from the normal curriculum (see the following discussion). If periodic institutional testing is to be done, it should always be done at the same time of year (beginning or end). Data obtained from this type of testing should be interpreted carefully. The Fitnessgram advisers discourage the use of Fitnessgram for determining student grades, long-term student achievement, or teacher success. As noted elsewhere in this manual, many factors other than physical activity influence fitness, so fitness tests are not good indicators of student achievement. See the chapter on factors that influence fitness in the online reference guide for more detailed explanations of this point.

• **Parental reporting and feedback.** The Fitnessgram software now offers a specific report for parents. This parent report includes easy-to-understand information on why their children are taking the Fitnessgram tests, their children's results, the Healthy Fitness Zone, suggestions for helping their children improve, why physical activity is important, and how regular physical activity leads to improved health and fitness. Both the student and parent reports can be printed in Spanish.

• **Personal tracking.** Personal tracking is another way of using Fitnessgram. Student test results are plotted on a regular basis to see whether children retain their fitness status over time. The goal is to help all youth meet or exceed criterion-referenced standards on all parts of fitness over time. When dramatic changes in personal performance occur, tracking will help the student, the teacher, and the parent identify reasons for changes. Self-testing results or institutional testing results can be used for tracking (see the *Fitnessgram/Activity-gram Test Administration Manual, Updated Third Edition*).

Uses of Fitnessgram that are consistent with the HELP philosophy are encouraged. Sometimes, however, methods of using fitness tests violate the HELP philosophy. Such uses are considered inappropriate practice and are discouraged. Among the practices that the Fitnessgram Advisory Council considers inappropriate are the following:

• *Using fitness test results as a primary method of grading students in physical education.* The Fitnessgram Advisory Council encourages teachers to evaluate students on their ability to self-administer fitness tests and interpret their personal results rather than on their test scores. Many factors other than physical activity done in physical education (or elsewhere) influence fitness test results (see the online reference guide chapter on factors influencing fitness). Those who engage in regular physical activity and still do not do well on fitness tests are turned off to physical activity when fitness determines their grades. Furthermore, having fitness scores in the healthy fitness zone rather than having extremely high fitness scores is the goal; thus, students should not be graded down if their scores are in the healthy fitness zone but not equal to others in a class.

• *Using student fitness scores as a measure of student or teacher success.* Educational leaders have recently developed achievement tests in a variety of areas (math, science, reading, and so on). In some cases these leaders have sought to develop tests for assessing student achievement in physical education. Using physical fitness scores as an indicator of student achievement is considered an inappropriate practice for several reasons, especially if teacher success is linked to student fitness test performance: (1) fitness does not correlate well with time spent in activity (Morrow & Freedson, 1994; Morrow, Jackson, & Payne, 1999), (2) many factors other than what is done in physical education class influence fitness, (3) when teacher success is based on student fitness performance, class sessions can resemble fitness training rather than physical education, resulting in a dislike of activity, and (4) when teacher success is based on student fitness performance, cheating on fitness tests becomes a problem, as it has in academic areas.

The following are answers to some commonly asked questions regarding Fitnessgram and Activitygram.

At what grade levels is the Fitnessgram battery intended to be used?

Students may begin learning about the Fitnessgram tests as early as the first grade. At this level, self-testing is encouraged as teachers begin to familiarize students with the test items and help them learn about the various parts of physical fitness. More formal testing is not recommended until the fourth grade. Standards of performance are not reliable before this age nor is student understanding of the meaning of results.

Do all Fitnessgram tests have to be given at each session of testing?

Not all Fitnessgram tests need to be given every time an assessment is done. One reasonable approach is to test youth, or have them test themselves, on the part of fitness that they are studying at a particular time.

Are pre- and posttesting recommended?

Some teachers think that tests at the beginning of the year and again at the end of the year are good indicators of student achievement. Although this type of testing may be used, the results must be interpreted with caution. First, students will improve whether they are engaging in activity or not, simply because they are getting older. Second, students learn over time to underperform on initial tests and perform at their best level on later tests if grades are based on improvement.

The Fitnessgram Advisory Council recommends that students receive many opportunities to learn to self-test accurately. In addition, keeping logs of their fitness test results helps them set fitness and activity goals and helps them plan personal programs. After students become accomplished in self-testing, they can repeat testing periodically to assess personal improvement. Using pre- and posttests of fitness as a primary method of grading students is discouraged. Having students learn to self-test

mote participation in physical activity for a lifetime. Learning to self-monitor physical activity helps students see how active they really are and helps them set goals for planning lifetime activity programs. Self-monitoring, goal setting, and program planning are considered self-management skills, and learning self-management skills is essential to lifetime physical activity adherence (Dale, Corbin, & Cuddihy, 1998; Dale & Corbin, 2000). Activitygram is a tool to aid in effective learning of self-management skills.

and keep records for goal setting and program planning is encouraged.

How is Activitygram intended to be used?

Activitygram was designed to help youth learn to self-monitor their personal physical activity patterns. The primary goal of both Fitnessgram and Activitygram is to encourage health and pro-

Like Fitnessgram, Activitygram can be used for institutional testing. Activitygram can also be used as a means of assessing activity patterns for research purposes.

Corbin, C.B. & Pangrazi, R.P. (2002). Fitnessgram and Activitygram: What are they? In G.J. Welk, J.R.J. Morrow, & H.B. Falls (Eds.), *Fitnessgram Reference Guide* (pp. Internet Resource). Dallas, TX: The Cooper Institute. Reprinted with permission from The Cooper Institute.

Health-Related Fitness Tests for Persons With Disabilities

Fitnessgram tests can be modified for students with disabilities. Information on how to do this is found in chapter 4 in a section titled "Considerations for Testing Special Populations" of the *Fitnessgram/Activitygram Test Administration Manual, Updated 3rd Edition.* As a complement to Fitnessgram, the Brockport Physical Fitness Test is specifically designed to test the health-related fitness of people with a wide range of physical and mental disabilities (Winnick & Short, 1999). The Brockport tests were developed through Project Target, a research study funded by the U.S. Department of Education.

The Brockport Physical Fitness Test resources include the following:

- *Brockport Physical Fitness Test Manual*
- *Brockport Physical Fitness Training Guide*
- *Brockport Physical Fitness Test Administration Video*
- Fitness Challenge software

For more information or to order the Brockport Physical Fitness Test Kit or materials, contact Human Kinetics at 800-747-4457 or on the Web at www.HumanKinetics.com.

Reprinted, by permission, from National Association for Sport and Physical Education (NASPE), 2005, *Physical education for lifelong fitness: The Physical Best teacher's guide,* 2nd ed. (Champaign, IL: Human Kinetics), 233.

Psychomotor Domain Assessment Examples

We have placed a number of psychomotor domain assessment examples in appendix C. These include one for motor skill development at the elementary level, one for assessing bench press technique, and a series of assessments for volleyball skills.

Affective Domain

The affective domain addresses the various emotions and feelings that students have toward PE. Teachers and parents who know how students feel now about PE can better help them become healthy, active adults later in life. Figure 10.1, figure 10.2, and figure 10.3 are examples of affective assessment.

1. I would rather exercise or play sports than watch TV.

   ☐ Yes   ☐ No

2. People who exercise regularly seem to have a lot of fun doing it.

   ☐ Yes   ☐ No

3. In school I look forward to attending physical education class.

   ☐ Yes   ☐ No

4. During physical education class at school I usually work up a sweat.

   ☐ Yes   ☐ No

5. When I grow up I will probably be too busy to stay physically fit.

   ☐ Yes   ☐ No

6. How do you feel about your ability to strike a ball with a racket?

   ☐ ☺   ☐ 😐   ☐ ☹

7. How do you feel about your ability to kick a ball hard and hit a target?

   ☐ ☺   ☐ 😐   ☐ ☹

8. How do you feel about your ability to run a long distance without stopping?

   ☐ ☺   ☐ 😐   ☐ ☹

9. How do you feel about your ability to play many different games and sports?

   ☐ ☺   ☐ 😐   ☐ ☹

10. How do you feel about your ability to participate in gymnastics?

    ☐ ☺   ☐ 😐   ☐ ☹

11. How do you feel about your ability to participate in dance?

    ☐ ☺   ☐ 😐   ☐ ☹

Figure 10.1 An example of an affective assessment tool.

Reprinted, by permission, from G. Graham, 2001, *Teaching children physical education: Becoming a master teacher*, 2nd ed. (Champaign, IL: Human Kinetics), 190.

Self-Grading Scorecard

Level	Behavior	Self-grade	Teacher grade
I	Does not call others names	_____	_____
I	Controls temper	_____	_____
I	Does not disrupt class	_____	_____
II	On time to class	_____	_____
II	Tries new activities	_____	_____
II	Listens to instructions	_____	_____
III	Makes and follows contract	_____	_____
III	Writes in journal every day	_____	_____
IV	Shares equipment	_____	_____
IV	Treats others kindly	_____	_____
IV	Shows good sportsmanship	_____	_____

Figure 10.2 An example of affective assessment, using a scorecard format.

Adapted, by permission, from D. Hellison, 1985, *Goals and strategies for teaching physical education*. (Champaign, IL: Human Kinetics), 21.

Assess yourself in physical education today!

What level are you at?

Level 3

- I gave my best effort in all activities today.
- I worked with my partner really well and encouraged him or her to do well.
- I worked with my group well and made sure that everyone got involved.
- I said only positive comments today.

Level 2

- I gave mostly my best effort in all activities today.
- I worked with my partner sufficiently and encouraged him or her most of the time.
- I worked with my group just enough to get by.
- I said mostly positive comments today.

Level 1

- I gave my best effort when I was successful only.
- I did not work well with my partner today.
- I worked with my group when it would benefit me the most.
- I did not say any positive comments today.

Figure 10.3 An example of affective assessment, asking students to assess themselves by identifying the level they are at in PE.

Used with permission of Jo Dixon and Audrey Satterblom.

Cognitive Domain

The cognitive domain covers students' ability to know and clearly communicate solutions to problems. There are many ways to assess stu-

dents' knowledge and understanding about PE activities; see figure 10.4 for just a few examples of cognitive assessment. Also, go to appendix C to see two examples of cognitive assessment for volleyball and two examples for weight training.

a

Name _____

Grade: _____4_____

1. When I run for a long time my heart
   (a) beats slower
   (b) stays the same
   (c) beats faster
   (d) almost stops

2. Which of the following is an example of muscular strength?
   (a) playing soccer
   (b) lifting a 50-pound bag of dog food
   (c) doing the sit-and-reach test
   (d) jumping rope

3. Being physically active is
   (a) fun
   (b) good for my heart
   (c) a way to stay well
   (d) all of the above

b

Name _____

Grade: _____7_____

1. Target heart rate means
   (a) the rate you always want your heart to beat
   (b) the maximum heart rate you can achieve
   (c) the ideal heart rate at which to work out to improve aerobic endurance
   (d) the lowest rate your heart can go

2. Which of the following is an example of muscular strength?
   (a) running a mile
   (b) bench-pressing 150 pounds one time
   (c) doing 35 push-ups
   (d) riding an exercise bike for 30 minutes

3. To gain basic health benefits from physical activity you must participate in
   (a) three or more sessions per week
   (b) activities lasting 20 minutes or more
   (c) moderate to vigorous activity
   (d) all of the above

c

Name _____

Grade: _____10_____

1. Determine the target heart rate for a person who is 17 years old (please show your work):

2. Define muscular strength and provide an example:

3. List five benefits of regular participation in physical activity:

Figure 10.4 Samples of written tests for different grade levels.

Portfolios

Using portfolios is not considered an assessment method. Because student portfolios are usually assembled from several assessments using multiple assessment modes, they are considered devices for collecting and communicating about student learning and teaching competence. A portfolio is an ongoing feedback system that documents student learning through exhibits and work samples. Although a portfolio can be assessed as a whole, its true purpose is to enrich the ability to learn, the desire to learn, and the learning itself. Students are involved in selecting and judging the quality of their own work. For complete details on creating a portfolio system for your students, see *Professional and Student Portfolios for Physical Education, Second Edition* by Melograno (2006).

Rubrics

A rubric is a list of statements explaining in detail the possible levels of performance for each criterion involved in an assessment task. As opposed to a checklist, in which criteria are evaluated by a simple yes or no judgment, a rubric may describe each criterion according to three, four, or even more levels of judgment. Depending on the nature and complexity of the task, rubrics can be holistic or analytical as well as task specific or generic (Hopple, 2005).

Holistic rubrics generally are applied to evaluate the overall quality of a student's work (see figure 10.5). In contrast, analytical rubrics allow the separation of specific criteria important to the evaluation of an assessment task. An example of an analytic rubric for a gymnastics performance for grades 1 and 2 is shown in figure 10.6. This example is considered a task-specific rubric because the wording in each descriptor reflects the unique nature of the gymnastics sequence that it measures. On the other hand, a generic rubric can apply to the evaluation of a variety of assessment tasks. An example is shown in figure 10.7.

Another example of a task-specific rubric can be seen in figure 10.8. Another example of a generic rubric can be seen in figure 10.9 (responsibility rubric).

The creation of rubrics is important for several reasons. Rubrics provide fairness in class because students will know ahead of time what they need to accomplish to earn a certain grade or other type of score. Rubrics also provide greater accountability and objectivity. If a parent asks why her or his child received a C in physical education, for example, the teacher can show the parent the rubrics for the assessments in class. This approach promotes an objective conversation rather than a potentially emotional one. Good rubrics are an important part of the educational process. They can make the assessment experience a

Level 4	Level 3	Level 2	Level 1	Level 0
• Helping others without being asked • Being partners with more than just my friends • Doing kind deeds for others • Always being safe	• Always doing my work • Trying my hardest • Taking care of equipment • Working nicely with others • Including everyone	• Trying my best only some of the time • Doing my work only sometimes • Needing reminders about my behavior and care of equipment	• Not doing my work • Not taking care of equipment • Not following directions • Saying "I can't" • Talking while others are talking	• Bothering others • Hurting others' feelings • Acting disrespectful • Choosing not to participate • Not being safe with self, others, or equipment

Figure 10.5 An example of a holistic rubric.

Reprinted, by permission, from C.J. Hopple, 2005, *Elementary physical education teaching & assessment: A practical guide,* 2nd ed. (Champaign, IL: Human Kinetics), 17.

Analytic Rubric for a Gymnastics Performance

Name _____ Class _____

___ How well did you perform the skills in your sequence? (Did you remember the hints to help you do your skills well?)

    3 points: You were able to perform each skill in your sequence correctly; you stretched your body parts to make them look good!

    2 points: You were able to perform most of the skills in your sequence correctly.

    1 point: You were able to perform some of the skills in your sequence correctly.

    0 points: You weren't able to perform any of the skills in your sequence correctly.

___ Did your sequence flow smoothly? Did you correctly remember the sequence that you made up?

    3 points: Your sequence was very smooth, and you remembered it correctly.

    2 points: Your sequence was pretty smooth, but you may have had a few small stops. You correctly remembered your sequence.

    1 point: Your sequence was somewhat smooth, but you had some stops. You may have forgotten some of your sequence.

    0 points: Your sequence was not smooth at all—you had many stops. You forgot the sequence that you wrote down.

___ Did you remember all the parts of your sequence?

	Yes (3 points)	No (0 points)
Includes at least one roll	____	____
Includes at least one balance	____	____
Includes at least one weight transfer	____	____
Has an ending shape	____	____

___ Total points

18: Congratulations! You practiced well—you are an Olympic gymnast!

16–17: Great job! You worked hard during class, and it shows—you are a terrific tumbler!

7–15: You did OK, but you need to improve a little more. You can do it; keep practicing! You are a junior gymnast!

0–6: You need to work a little harder; you can improve if you try! Practice at home or in the yard—you are on the practice team.

Figure 10.6 An example of an analytic rubric.

Reprinted, by permission, from C.J. Hopple, 2005, *Elementary physical education teaching & assessment: A practical guide,* 2nd ed. (Champaign, IL: Human Kinetics), 18.

Competent	Achieving	Needs practice
• Student is able to create space consistently by moving to open spaces to successfully pass object; pass is not broken up by defender; student does not need to be reminded by teacher or teammates to move. • Student consistently creates space by moving to open space to receive object; needs no reminders to move to open space. • Student is able to move body between object and goal consistently; is consistently in close position to make a play on the object or break up the play.	• Student sometimes, but not always, moves to open spaces to pass an object; many times, pass is blocked by guarding defender. • Student sometimes, but not always, moves to open space to receive object; at times, stands in location where first moved, no matter where teammates or defense have moved; may need prompting by teammates or teacher to move to open area. • Student sometimes, but not always, moves body between object and goal; at times, is not in correct position to make a play on the object or break up the play.	• Student does not grasp the concept of moving to open spaces to pass an object; does not attempt to move away from guarding defender. • Student does not grasp concept of moving to open space to receive object; does not attempt to move away from defender to receive object from teammate. • Student is rarely able to move body between object and goal; consistently gets beat out of position by offense.

Figure 10.7 An example of a generic rubric.

Reprinted, by permission, from C.J. Hopple, 2005, *Elementary physical education teaching & assessment: A practical guide,* 2nd ed. (Champaign, IL: Human Kinetics), 19.

positive one for students and improve communication with parents and other stakeholders.

Grading

According to NASPE (2005c), "In an ideal world, you would not have to assign a grade. Each grading period, you would have plenty of prep time to write detailed reports of each student's current fitness status. Then you would sit down for an hour or two with each parent and student to communicate this information in full, set goals, and help develop plans to meet those goals—in a private, quiet, and comfortable office."

Unfortunately you are most likely in a school that requires grades for physical education but does not allocate enough time to provide the detailed information just described. Debate continues about how to weight grades in physical education. For example, should you grade on the process (uses the correct technique for shooting free throws) or the product

(makes a high percentage of free throws regardless of correct technique)? Should you grade on skill level or improvement? Should you grade on effort or results? Should you put more emphasis on written tests or skills tests? Should dressing out or taking a shower be figured into a student's physical education grade?

The specifics of how you grade will depend on district and school policy as well as departmental policy. Ideally, a physical education grade will be based on a variety of factors and in the end measure progress toward acquiring the knowledge, skills, and appreciation needed to live an active, healthy life.

You must make sure that your grading system is fair, and that students and parents understand it, at the beginning of the school year. Figure 10.10 is an example of providing expectations and the grading policy to students and parents at the beginning of the year.

Figure 10.11 is an example of an interim report so that parents can help correct an issue before it shows in a grade.

Scoring Rubric for Kindergarten Children on the Underhand Throw

Achieving

- Always faces target when throwing underhand
- Always swings arm back ("tick")
- Always swings arm forward ("tock")
- Always steps with the opposite foot
- Always watches the target

Developing

- Sometimes faces target when throwing underhand
- Sometimes swings arm back ("tick")
- Sometimes swings arm forward ("tock")
- Sometimes steps with the opposite foot
- Sometimes watches the target

Not yet

- Does not face target when throwing underhand
- Does not swing arm back ("tick")
- Does not swing arm forward ("tock")
- Does not step with the opposite foot
- Does not watch the target

Figure 10.8 An example of a task-specific rubric.

Reprinted, by permission, from L. Ardovino and S. Sanders, 1997, "The development of a physical education assessment report," *Teaching Elementary Physical Education,* 8(3): 23-25.

Responsibility Rubric

	Consistently	Sporadically	Seldom	Never
Contributes to own well-being:				
Effort and self-motivation				
Independence				
Goal setting				
Contributes to others' well-being:				
Respect				
Helping				

Figure 10.9 An example of a generic rubric for responsibility.

Reprinted, by permission, from D. Hellison, 2003, *Teaching responsibility through physical activity,* 2nd ed. (Champaign, IL: Human Kinetics), 111.

Physical Education Expectations

The Grundy Center Physical Education Department, in partnership with PE4life, Polar, and the University of Northern Iowa, challenges students to make regular exercise part of their daily routine. During the past decade, many concerns have surfaced regarding the health of today's youth and the effects of physical inactivity. Therefore, the focus in PE has turned to fitness and wellness, allowing all students, regardless of athletic ability, to become interested in their personal well-being.

Expectations of Physical Education Students in Grades 9 Through 12

1. Class attendance—daily attendance and participation is required!

   - For an absence to be excused, students must bring a note from a parent or a doctor's office, or the parent or doctor must call the high school office to confirm the excuse.

   - Two excused absences are allowed. After the second absence, students must make up class in one of two ways:

     1. Working out in the fitness room Monday through Friday (mornings 6:00–7:30 or after school 3:30–5:00) and then meeting with the physical education instructor to earn your points.

     2. Attending the monthly Healthy Living seminar. Your attendance and a one-page, double-spaced reflection paper will make up a missed class period.

   - Students who have missed class are responsible for initiating the process to complete missed classes, assignments, or other work.

   - If a student is absent from class and the absence is unexcused, the result will be 0 (zero) points for that day. Students do not have the opportunity to make up participation or test points.

2. Tardiness

   - Students are expected to be ready for class, with heart rate monitors on, five minutes after the tardy bell rings.

   - Students are expected to be in the locker room before the tardy bell rings.

   - Any student who enters class after class has begun will be marked tardy.

   - Each set of three tardies during the trimester will lower your final trimester grade one-third of a letter grade.

3. Lockers and locker room

   - Each student will be given a lock and locker. Do not share!

   - The locker gives you a place to secure your belongings.

   - Lock up your belongings during class time. Do not leave valuables unlocked at any time.

   - If you have a problem, please speak to one of the instructors.

4. Class attire

   - Students must wear an appropriate T-shirt, gym shorts, tennis shoes, and socks. PE clothes must be something different from what you are wearing to school!

Figure 10.10 A sample of written student expectations. *(continued)*

- Students who choose to wear their school clothes as their physical education uniform will face the following consequences:
  1. First offense: Students will be allowed to participate without penalty.
  2. Second offense: Students will be allowed to participate, and parents will be notified.
  3. Third offense: A conference involving the student, a parent, the teacher, and the principal will be scheduled to address the problem.

5. Grading guidelines

   Grading scale

90–100	A
80–89	B
70–79	C
60–69	D
0–59	F

The following criteria will be used to assess students throughout the trimester:

Effort: 50 percent

- One-half of each day's grades will be based on your effort. Heart rate monitors will be used to provide evidence of your effort.
- Each student will be assigned a transmitter and wrist monitor.
- Each student is responsible for his or her own chest strap.

Daily participation: 20 percent

- Students will be graded on being focused and on task, having a positive attitude, and displaying good behavior.
- See rubric for daily participation on HSPE link at the PE4life Web site.

Skills: 15 percent

- Students will be assessed on their demonstration of skills for each unit of instruction.

Knowledge tests: 15 percent

- A written exam will be given at the end of each unit of instruction.

6. Class format
   - Each class period will include the following:
     1. Concept of the day
     2. Warm-up
     3. Dynamic stretching
     4. Unit of activity
     5. Cool-down and review of concept

7. Time schedules

First period	8:10-9:22
Second period	9:30-10:41
Third period	10:45-12:10

Please stay in the gym until the dismissal bell rings at the end of each period. Being in the hallway is unacceptable!

Figure 10.10 *(continued)*

Physical Education Interim Report

Washington Elementary School

Name _____ Class _____

Dear Parent or Guardian:

During the first part of this grading period, your child has had difficulty with the following (checked) skills or behaviors:

- Not bringing shoes to class
- Not completing homework assignments or not turning them in
- Being disrespectful to others in class
- Not participating in class activities
- Not completing class assignments

Continued difficulty may cause your child to receive a less than satisfactory grade in physical education on his or her report card for the nine weeks. Please contact me at school (123-4567) to set up a time when we can meet in person or talk on the phone so that we can help your child be successful in physical education.

Thank you,
Christine Hopple
Physical education teacher

Figure 10.11 A sample of an interim report.

Reprinted, by permission, from C.J. Hopple, 2005, *Elementary physical education teaching & assessment: A practical guide,* 2nd ed. (Champaign, IL: Human Kinetics), 47.

Nutrition Resources

Nutrition Curriculum Lessons

Family Nutrition Education Resources: Nutrition and Lifeskills for Families
(University of Missouri Extension)

This site provides introductory lessons to MyPyramid appropriate for grades pre-K–8.
http://outreach.missouri.edu/fnep/teaching.htm

Food and Nutrition Resources for Teachers
(Food and Nutrition Information Centers)

Find a variety of lesson plans and curricula as well as organizations and companies that provide nutrition education materials and resources for audiences from young to old.
www.nalusda.gov/fnic/educators.html
www.nal.usda.gov/fnic/etext/000045.html

Nutrition Across the Curriculum: Lesson Plans for Grades Pre-K–12
(Louisiana Department of Education)

This site offers a compilation of nutrition lessons that have been correlated to standards and benchmarks set by the Louisiana Department of Education in health, physical education, science, mathematics, English and language arts, and social studies. These lessons are designed to be an enhancement for teaching and learning across the curriculum that will result in positive behavior change.
www.doe.state.la.us/lde/nutrition/1667.html

Nutrition Explorations
(National Dairy Council)

The site is sponsored by the National Dairy Council and provides a fun and easy way to teach and learn nutrition through interactive lesson plans, activities, and games for teachers, parents, kids, and food-service personnel.
www.nutritionexplorations.org

PE Central

This site provides an extensive database of ready-to-use, interactive health and physical activity lesson plans designed for grades pre-K through 12, and is geared specifically toward physical education and classroom teachers.
www.pecentral.org
www.pecentral.org/lessonideas/searchresults.asp?category=58

Public Broadcasting System (PBS) Teacher Source

This site offers multidisciplinary lessons designed to help support core curriculum with content developed by the PBS Children's Hospital program and Web site. The curriculum addresses a variety of core subjects (including health) and is designed specifically for ninth- through twelfth-graders. The lessons allow discussion or assignments for varying lengths of time, from one class period to an entire school term.
www.pbs.org/teachersource/health_fitness/high-nutrition.html

General Information for Teachers

American Dietetic Association

This site provides science-based nutrition and diet information you can trust.
www.eatright.org

Dietary Guidelines for Americans
(HHS, USDA)

Published every five years by HHS and USDA, these guidelines are the official position of these U.S. government agencies on sensible nutrition for people two years and older.
www.healthierus.gov/dietaryguidelines/

Healthy Youth: Nutrition
(Center for Chronic Disease Prevention and Health Promotion)

The CDC addresses six critical types of adolescent health behavior that research shows contribute to the leading causes of death and disability among adults and youth. The site provides helpful resources such as data and statistics, science-based strategies, policy guidance, and local, state, and federal support. www.cdc.gov/HealthyYouth/nutrition/index.htm

MyPyramid.gov *(Department of Agriculture)*

This official USDA site utilizes interactive and educational tools and games to introduce the new food pyramid. MyPyramid is part of an overall food guidance system that emphasizes the need for a more individualized approach to improving diet and lifestyle. The MyPyramid for kids link provides tailored lessons, materials, and games for elementary-school-aged children. www.mypyramid.gov

National 5 A Day *(HHS, NIH, NCI)*

Five A Day for Better Health is a national nutrition program sponsored by the National Cancer Institute. It is designed to encourage Americans to eat five or more servings of fruits and vegetables every day. The links take you through the site, which presents details about the fruit and vegetable industries, recipes and tips, and corresponding state programs. www.5aday.gov

Carol M. White Physical Education Program *(U.S. Department of Education)*

The Carol M. White PEP Web site highlights a number of nutrition teaching resources under the subject of Health and Safety. The Web site provides excellent information from the Department of Agriculture, Centers for Disease Control and Prevention, and the Department of Health and Human Services on a variety of topics, including eating out, fruit and vegetable consumption, recommendations to help schools implement health programs, policies that promote healthy behaviors among youth, sample menus, dietary guidelines, instructional strategies, and a host of other nutrition-related topics. www.ed.gov/programs/whitephysed/index.html

Centers for Disease Control and Prevention (CDC)

The CDC nutrition resources cover a variety of topics, consisting of several featured items that help you sort through all of the information available about nutrition and food choices. In addition, the CDC site helps you learn more about how healthy eating and physical activity promote weight maintenance. The site also provides a comprehensive collection of resources designed to assist health professionals, including key reports, recommendations, and surveillance data. Another featured item provides information on healthy youth nutrition topics, which highlight school nutrition programs and policies related to adolescent nutrition and health. www.cdc.gov/nccdphp/dnpa/nutrition/index.htm

Tools

Food Label Education Tools and General Information *(U.S. Food and Drug Administration/CFSAN)*

This site provided by the U.S. Food and Drug Administration offers historical information, label education tools, and educational programs for understanding and interpreting food fact labels. www.cfsan.fda.gov/~dms/lab-gen.html

Nutrition Analysis Tool (NATS)

You can utilize this online food analyzer for nutritional composition information for many common foods and beverages. http://nat.crgq.com/

USDA Nutrient Database

This government site provides an Internet reference tool produced by the U.S. Department of Agriculture. Users can search the USDA Nutrient Database for the nutritional value of almost any food item. www.rahul.net/cgi-bin/fatfree/usda/usda.cgi

Weight Loss Resource.com

This commercial site offers several useful tools for determining exercise expenditure, caloric intake, and body mass index calculations. www.weightlossresource.com/tools

PE4life Resources

PE4life Tools and Resources

PE4life is here to help. We want to be your teammate every step of the way. Here are some resources to help you get started.

www.pe4life.org

The PE4life Web site is a tremendous resource for anyone interested in the issue of physical activity for children and the role of physical education. The site contains advocacy tools, research information, current news, video footage, photos, audio, a discussion forum, and information about the Carol M. White Physical Education Program (PEP) grants. Most importantly, it provides information on how to register to train at a PE4life Academy. It also provides follow-up support for community and school teams that have gone through training.

Community Action Kit

Use the PE4life Community Action Kit video, presentations, and handouts included on the DVD that is packaged in this book to make the case for quality, daily physical education with the key stakeholders in your community.

PE4life Summits

PE4life hosts a number of summits throughout the country on topics such as combating childhood obesity. These events feature presentations by respected physical education professionals, as well as PE advocates from the education, health care, and business and government sectors. Visit the PE4life Web site at www.pe4life.org for information on an upcoming PE4life Summit in your region.

National PE Day®

National PE Day® occurs during the first week of May each year and celebrates the value and importance of quality PE programs. PE4life hosts a national event in Washington, DC, in partnership with the Sporting Goods Manufacturers Association (SGMA). A key part of National PE Day is a major advocacy effort on behalf of the entire physical education industry with members of Congress in our nation's capital. Information and resources for celebrating National PE Day in your own community are available at www.pe4life.org.

PEP Federal Grant Program

PE4life is a driving force behind the Carol M. White Physical Education Program (PEP), which awards grant money to schools throughout the country through the U.S. Department of Education to enrich and expand physical education programs by providing training and equipment. A helpful brochure titled "So . . . You Want to Apply for a PEP Grant" is available for download from the PE4life Web site.

National PE Day®: Celebrities and Athletes Help Spread the Message

Each year, schools and communities nationwide celebrate National PE Day® in a show of support for physical education and the positive role that it plays in fighting the childhood obesity epidemic and helping children lead active, healthy lifestyles. The commemorative day, launched by PE4life in 2001, coincides with an intense advocacy effort on Capitol Hill in Washington, DC, led by PE4life and other physical education advocates. Meetings are held with members of Congress to encourage them to support physical education in a variety of ways. The meetings feature celebrity athletes who are passionate about increasing physical education opportunities for kids. A key outcome of these meetings has been increased funding for the Carol M. White

Physical Education Program (PEP) grants. Over $325 million in total grants have been distributed since 2001. Here is a list of celebrity athletes who have helped PE4life in this effort since 2001:

2001: Miss America Angie Perez-Baraquio, Herschel Walker

2002: Denise Austin, Dominique Dawes, Donna de Varona, Mike Kohn, Martina Navratilova

2003: Tori Allen, Tiki Barber, John Calipari, Mia Hamm, Larry Holmes, Jackie Joyner-Kersee, Mike Kohn, Archie Manning, Peyton Manning, Gary Williams

2004: Tori Allen, Tommy Amaker, Jennifer Azzi, Chris Byrd, Cory Everson, Billie Jean King, James Leija, Carl Lewis, Stacey Nuveman, Clinton Portis, Coach John Thompson, Herschel Walker

2005: Teddy Atlas, Jennifer Azzi, Alana Beard, Tim Brown, Peyton Manning, Archie Manning, Heather Mitts, Bill Russell, Stan Smith, Tubby Smith, Herschel Walker, Trey Wingo, Steve Young

2006: Freddie Adu, Jennifer Azzi, Alana Beard, Tim Brown, Jennifer Capriati, Alecko Eskandarian, Patrick Kerney, Jim Larranaga, Peter Manfredo, Jr., Archie Manning, Kerry McCoy, Lawrence Moten, Antwaan Randel El, Tiffany Roberts, Bill Russell, Herschel Walker, Kellen Winslow

Parent Survey

The following sample survey will help you assess parents' attitudes toward your school's current PE program. (This is also found on the DVD, where you can print it out.)

Note to PE4life Academy participants: The following survey will help you understand how parents feel about your current physical education program and gauge the support that you will have as you begin developing your PE4life program. We encourage you to use this survey template and adapt it as needed to assess attitudes toward your school's PE program. **You can download the survey from the PE4life Web site at www.pe4life.org.**

[SCHOOL NAME] is evaluating its physical education program and considering making a variety of improvements and changes to better meet the health and wellness needs of students. We appreciate your taking the time to answer the following questions and provide feedback to the physical education department.

Please circle a number from 1 to 5 to indicate how you feel about the various programs or components of [SCHOOL NAME'S] current physical education program.

1—Very dissatisfied

2—Somewhat dissatisfied

3—Satisfied

4—Very satisfied

5—Extremely satisfied

NF—Not familiar with this program or component

1. How satisfied are you with the variety and types of activities that your child is exposed to in his or her PE class at [SCHOOL NAME]?

    1   2   3   4   5   NF

2. How satisfied are you that [SCHOOL NAME'S] PE classes focus on students of all skill levels?

 1 2 3 4 5 NF

3. How satisfied are you that [SCHOOL NAME'S] physical education program effectively incorporates nutrition education into PE class?

 1 2 3 4 5 NF

4. How satisfied are you with the current PE facilities at [SCHOOL NAME]?

 1 2 3 4 5 NF

5. How satisfied are you that [SCHOOL NAME'S] current PE program is addressing your child's lifetime health and wellness?

 1 2 3 4 5 NF

6. How satisfied are you that [SCHOOL NAME] effectively uses technology (e.g., heart rate monitors, fitness equipment, and so on) to facilitate activities and lessons taught in PE class?

 1 2 3 4 5 NF

7. How satisfied are you that your child receives individual assessment of his or her fitness progress?

 1 2 3 4 5 NF

8. How satisfied are you with the grading process for PE at [SCHOOL NAME]?

 1 2 3 4 5 NF

9. Overall, how satisfied are you with the PE program at [SCHOOL NAME]?

 1 2 3 4 5 NF

10. How satisfied are you that physical education, as it is conducted today, is an important part of your child's education at [SCHOOL NAME]?

 1 2 3 4 5 NF

11. How satisfied are you that your child gets enough physical activity on a daily basis?

 1 2 3 4 5 NF

12. How satisfied are you that daily PE class is a part of your child's education at [SCHOOL NAME]?

 1 2 3 4 5 NF

Please provide any additional comments or suggestions about the physical education program at [SCHOOL NAME] in the space below.

_____

_____

Thank you for taking the time to complete this survey.

We will keep you updated about our plans for [SCHOOL NAME'S] PE program and will continue to ask for your feedback and suggestions for improvement.

From *PE4life: Developing and Promoting Quality Physical Education,* by PE4life, 2007, Champaign, IL: Human Kinetics.

Fitness Comparison

Student fitness can be influenced by many factors outside a school's control, including heredity, parent involvement, and activity opportunities in the communities. However, quality physical education can make a difference. Naperville, Illinois, made a commitment to quality physical education and became a PE4life Academy, and a large number of students there have made it into the Healthy Fitness Zone (the health-related criteria established by Fitnessgram). See figure 1, which shows the percentage of Naperville students in the Healthy Fitness Zone as compared to students in California (this population is being used here because a large data set is available).

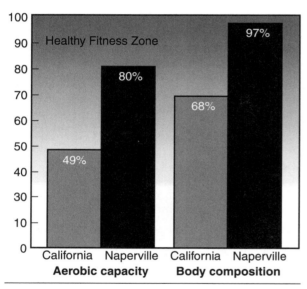

Figure 1 PE4life Academy (Naperville, Illinois) versus State of California.

PE4life Academy Testimonials

The following quotations represent individual reactions to the PE4life program and its results.

"The focus of [our] program was shifted toward the idea of individuals learning healthy habits to live a healthy life."

Tim McCord, health and physical education department chair, Titusville (Pennsylvania) Area School District

"Our physical education program at Deer Path has changed. We have made a shift from a skill-based curriculum to a fitness-based curriculum. This does not mean we have taken sports out of the curriculum but [we have] modified their concepts to be fitness orientated."

Bob Van Kast, wellness department chairperson, Deer Path Middle School East, Lake Forest, Illinois

"I returned to Kingman loaded with enthusiasm and 'ammunition' to present to my principal and superintendent."

Sandi Minkler, physical education department head, Kingman (Arizona) Junior High School

"You will end up saving more lives through your profession as a physical education instructor than I will ever be able to do as a physician."

Dr. Michael Kretz

"You really inspired all three of our teachers who came to visit you."

Crystal Gorwitz, Hortonville (Wisconsin) Middle School

"I left a PE4life [Academy] with the feeling of a man on a mission. I'm proud to say our program has grown by leaps and bounds using the PE4life program as a model."

Bryan T. Schwab, health and physical education department chairperson, Oil City (Pennsylvania) Area School District

"PE4life is more than a program. It is a belief system that holds sacred the ideal and beliefs that every citizen—young or old, short or tall, slim or heavy, rich or poor—has the right to make healthy choices. To such an end, I hope and pray that we too, in days to come, might provide our learning community with many opportunities for mind and body wellness. But for all you pessimists we say you've just got to see it to believe it. PE4life is for real people in a real world and it should be considered for all levels of learners."

Dennis Ledebur, elementary principal, Titusville (Pennsylvania) Area School District

"My school district has received the PEP grant in 2003 and purchased new cardio equipment and heart rate monitors. The district is committed to a higher level of fitness for our students. It is our goal come September 2004 that our PE program will be a model for others to see, and that will be thanks to Rick Schupbach and PE4life."

Rhonda Ritz, Camden County technical schools, Pennsauken campus, Pennsauken, New Jersey

"Thank you for all the time and effort that you put into making my visit and training so successful. The training was very worthwhile and I have come home with more ideas than I thought was possible. My visit exceeded my expectations. Thank you!"

Chris Nordstrom, Epiphany School, Seattle, Washington

"You not only gave us the first step and vision to improve our program, you gave all of us a piece of your personal passion and your passion for our profession. Your knowledge and guidance will be a great help for us in taking the next steps toward creating a quality program. We hope our journey leads to a quality program such as yours."

Make Sinram, Waterloo (Iowa) Community Schools

"Your use of heart rate monitors with students every day as a form of assessment is impressive. Allowing every student to be evaluated on their effort and not their abilities is a key way to show students that they are not being judged on their physical abilities or judged against another student."

Amy Waters, Nashua Elementary School, North Kansas City, Missouri

"Our PE teachers are highly motivated to establish PE4life in our schools. You have a great thing going!"

Barb Opheim, school board member, Waterloo (Iowa) Community Schools

"Attending the PE4life [Academy] certainly raised the bar for us. I've never seen children so excited about coming to PE class. What is going on with physical education in [the PE4life Academy] should be happening in every school in America."

Pollia Griffin, assistant superintendent, Madison County School District, Flora, Mississippi, 2002 PEP grant winner

"I recently had the opportunity to spend the most exciting day at the PE4life [Academy] in Naperville, Illinois. If a day with the PE4life team does not get you fired up about the potential for physical education, you may want to go to the nurse's office and check your pulse.

PE4life did an amazing job of educating me on how to involve our entire communities in making sure our children have opportunities to build lifelong healthy habits. I was told to look beyond school budgets to health organizations, health clubs, the medical community and more, to help educate everyone in the community about the benefits of reducing childhood obesity and increasing good, healthy habits in children. Their [PE4life] experience has been a very excited involvement (and financing) from some surprising sources outside of the normal school supply chain. How can a physical education professional not get excited about *that!*"

Mark Dresser, vice president of catalog sales, Sportime

"Our visit to the PE4life [Academy] will have a major impact on how physical education will now be delivered in Grosse Ile. The shift to physical education for lifelong fitness behaviors and attitudes will have a positive impact on the future of children throughout the country. I can't help but think this is one of the most important days I have spent this year!"

Peter J. Dion, superintendent, Grosse Ile (Michigan) Township Schools

"At the PE4life [Academy], physical education teachers are regarded as leaders in health promotion and preventive medicine."

Nancy Bailey, health and PE resource teacher, Kansas City (Missouri) School District

"Of the many schools in our region (where my students could visit), I selected Grundy Center because I believe my students will be able to observe one of the best programs in the nation, in addition to being able to interact with one of our leading physical education teachers."

Rip Marston, professor, School of Health, Physical Education and Leisure Services, University of Northern Iowa, Cedar Falls, Iowa

"My son is going to college at Central in Pella. Would it be possible for him to see your program in action? I want him to learn from the best."

Bonnie Cobler,
Ottumwa (Iowa) Public Schools

Sample Press Release

Use this sample press release as a template for your own press release, modifying it to meet the unique aspects of your situation. You can download this form from the PE4life Web site at www.pe4life.org, or you can print it from the DVD included with this book.

Note to schools: Consider adding the following information as appropriate:

- How your program will be funded
- Any new facilities that will be built or new equipment that will be added
- Any new PE staff that will be hired
- Whether your new program will be a daily requirement

For Immediate Release
Media contacts:
[SCHOOL NAME]
[NAME OF TEACHER]
[PHONE NUMBER]
PE4life
Carrie Gibson, PE4life Academy Coordinator
cgibson@pe4life.org
816-472-7345, ext 133

[SCHOOL NAME] Makes Getting Fit Top Priority
New PE4life Program to Teach Kids of All Skill Levels
Lifetime Health and Wellness Practices
CITY, STATE, DATE—With the support of administrators, parents, members of the medical community, and the [SCHOOL DISTRICT] school board, [SCHOOL NAME] is adopting a new approach to physical education that will focus on teaching children lifetime health and wellness practices.

[SCHOOL NAME] aims to implement a PE4life program—which will emphasize the importance of quality, daily physical activity—by [DATE], according to physical education director [NAME].

"With the obesity rate climbing and inactivity among children becoming more commonplace, the health and wellness of our children are a top concern in our community," said [ABOVE NAME]. "We want to take a strong stance in favor of quality physical activity and refocus our program to emphasize fitness over athletics and to benefit children of all shapes and sizes."

[SCHOOL NAME]'s new PE program will embrace the following PE4life components:
- Creates the motivation and awareness in children to embrace health and fitness for a lifetime
- Introduces a variety of sports and fitness participation opportunities for children
- Provides fitness assessments for all children
- Utilizes technology in activities and assessments

"When we looked at all of the research connecting physical activity with brain development and academic success, we knew it was time to reevaluate our priorities and begin changing our approach to physical education," said [SCHOOL ADMINISTRATOR]. "Just as it is the responsibility of schools to teach our children lifelong skills in mathematics and reading comprehension, we believe it is our responsibility to provide students with habits to get active and stay active—for life."

The new physical education program at [SCHOOL NAME] is modeled after the PE4life Academy—an exemplary program that shows firsthand how to incorporate PE4life principles into school communities. [SCHOOL NAME]'s revamped physical education program will explore creative new activities to appeal to students of all sizes and skill levels, including [NAME SAMPLE ACTIVITIES, e.g., KAYAKING, ROCK CLIMBING, AND THE LIKE].

The program will also emphasize the use of technology—including heart rate monitors and other assessment tools—to evaluate students' progress based on health standards, not athletic standards. Students will be evaluated on their personal fitness progress and will be encouraged to adopt daily physical activity as part of their lives outside school.

"Quality, daily physical education prepares children to take personal responsibility for their own health and wellness and can have a tremendous impact on their overall quality of life," said Anne Flannery, president and CEO of PE4life. "[SCHOOL NAME]'s new program is the beginning of a lifelong learning process in which children learn how to live active and healthy lives."

About PE4life

Founded in January 2000, PE4life inspires active, healthy living by advancing the development of quality, daily physical education programs for all children. The organization's philosophy is that daily physical education provides an effective and efficient solution to the physical inactivity epidemic by fostering lifelong fitness habits and reducing children's exposure to chronic diseases. PE4life's goals for helping kids get active include raising awareness about the physical inactivity levels of America's youth and the state of physical education across the nation; promoting the need for reform of educational policy, including required standardized fitness and cognitive health and wellness tests for children in grades K through 12; promoting model quality physical education programs in every state; empowering physical educators, parents, and community leaders to become advocates for quality, daily physical education; and stimulating private and public funding for quality physical education programs.

From *PE4life: Developing and Promoting Quality Physical Education,* by PE4life, 2007, Champaign, IL: Human Kinetics.

National Association for Sport and Physical Education (NASPE) Standards

Physical activity is critical to the development and maintenance of good health. The goal of physical education is to develop physically educated individuals who have the knowledge, skills, and confidence to enjoy a lifetime of healthful physical activity.

A physically educated person:

Standard 1: Demonstrates competency in motor skills and movement patterns needed to perform a variety of physical activities.

Standard 2: Demonstrates understanding of movement concepts, principles, strategies, and tactics as they apply to the learning and performance of physical activities.

Standard 3: Participates regularly in physical activity.

Standard 4: Achieves and maintains a health-enhancing level of physical fitness.

Standard 5: Exhibits responsible personal and social behavior that respects self and others in physical activity settings.

Standard 6: Values physical activity for health, enjoyment, challenge, self-expression, and/or social interaction.

The National Association for Sport and Physical Education (NASPE)'s definition of Quality Physical Education is the following:

NASPE believes that every student in our nation's schools, from kindergarten through 12th grade, should have the opportunity to participate in quality physical education. It is the unique role of quality physical education programs to develop the health-related fitness, physical competence, and cognitive understanding about physical activity for all students so that they can adopt healthy and physically active lifestyles. Today's quality physical education programs provide learning experiences that meet the developmental needs of youngsters, which helps improve a child's mental alertness, academic performance, readiness to learn, and enthusiasm for learning. These are important factors when striving to achieve the overall school mission.

According to NASPE guidelines, a high-quality physical education program includes the following components:

- Opportunity to learn
- Meaningful content
- Appropriate instruction

Each of these areas is outlined in detail in NASPE's quality physical education (QPE) documents, including the following: the National Standards for Physical Education; Appropriate Practice Documents; Opportunity to Learn Documents; and the Assessment Series. These resources can be ordered online at www.aahperd.org or by calling 800-321-0789.

Opportunity to Learn

- Instructional periods totaling 150 minutes per week (elementary) and 225 minutes per week (middle and secondary school)
- Qualified physical education specialist providing a developmentally appropriate program
- Adequate equipment and facilities

Meaningful Content

- Instruction in a variety of motor skills designed to enhance the physical, mental, social, and emotional development of every child
- Fitness education and assessment to help children understand, improve, and maintain their physical well-being
- Development of cognitive concepts about motor skills and fitness
- Opportunities to improve children's emerging social and cooperative skills and gain a multicultural perspective
- Promotion of regular amounts of appropriate physical activity now and throughout life

Appropriate Instruction

- Full inclusion of all students
- Maximum practice opportunities for class activities
- Well-designed lessons that facilitate student learning
- Out-of-school assignments that support learning and practice
- No physical activity for punishment
- Uses regular assessment to monitor and reinforce student learning

What Constitutes a Quality Physical Education (2002), reprinted with permission from the National Association for Sport and Physical Education (NASPE), 1900 Association Drive, Reston, VA 20191-1599.
Available: www.aahperd.org/naspe/template.cfm?template=qualityPePrograms.html.

How Is a School Selected As a PE4life Academy?

A PE4life Academy is an exemplary, daily physical education program focused on lifetime, health-related physical activity and fitness. PE4life Academies provide training to school and community leaders with the objective of assisting them with the development of PE4life programs in their communities. To become a PE4life Academy, a team of people representing a school must complete training at a PE4life Academy site, submit an application, and meet the criteria to become a PE4life Certified Program. Next, a school must go through a rigorous qualification process that includes a commitment to providing PE4life Academy training to other schools, partnering with a research university, submitting to site inspections, complying with PE4life standards, and other specific academy criteria. For more information, contact the PE4life offices at 816-472-7345 or visit www.pe4life.org.

PE4Life Academy Recommended Attendees for Maximum Training Benefits

1. PE teacher
2. Superintendent
3. Medical doctor
4. Principal
5. Assistant principal
6. School board member or members
7. PTA president
8. Parent or parents (more than one preferred)
9. Medical profession (nurse and others)
10. School–business partners
11. Curriculum director
12. Technology director
13. School finance manager
14. Hospital CEO
15. Mayor
16. Newspaper reporters (city and student reporters)
17. Park district staff member
18. YMCA representative
19. Local health club owners
20. Students
21. Potential corporate sponsors from your community
22. College PE professor—local or one that provides student teachers
23. Retired physical education teacher (often has extra time and still has passion)

24. Health teacher
25. Politicians or policy makers—especially if one lives in your school district
    A. State school board member
    B. State representatives
    C. Federal senators or representatives
    D. County school board members
26. As many physical education staff as possible

Sources of Funding for Prevention Programs

Only two percent of the $1.8 trillion that the United States spends annually on health care goes toward prevention of chronic diseases. The following wellness programs provide funding for prevention.

- Carol M. White Physical Education Program: This program provides grants to local educational agencies and community-based organizations to initiate, expand, and improve physical education programs for students in kindergarten through 12th grade.

- Extramural Prevention Research: This funding is for public health research at the Centers for Disease Control and Prevention (CDC), to define the best strategies to motivate healthy lifestyles and communicate that information to communities.

- Mental Health Surveillance: Under this initiative, the Substance Abuse and Mental Health Services Administration (SAMHSA), in consultation with CDC, will develop ways of monitoring the mental health status of the population, the mental and behavioral health risks facing the nation, and the immediate and long-term effect of emergencies on mental health and behavior.

- Nutrition, Physical Activity, Obesity State Grants: This CDC state grant program will fund capacity-building activities, including efforts to develop state nutrition and physical activity plans, identify community resources and gaps, implement small-scale interventions, and raise public awareness of system changes needed to help state residents achieve and maintain a healthy weight.

- Obesity Research: This investment is for research into the causes of and cures for obesity, including the development of a strategic plan for National Institutes of Health (NIH) obesity research, which will coordinate NIH obesity research across all the Institutes.

- Pioneering Healthy Communities: Funding is included to support the YMCA of the USA for its work in developing healthier communities through its Pioneering Healthier Communities conference. This program will be a proactive response to the surging epidemic of obesity and physical inactivity by supporting community-based solutions to these problems.

- Prevention Centers: Prevention research centers are a network of academic centers, public health agencies, and community partners that are conducting applied research and practice in chronic disease prevention and control. These centers are working with communities to evaluate programs meant to encourage increased physical activity, reduce the prevalence of smoking, and foster better eating habits.

- School Mental Health Services: This program to support the integration of schools and mental health systems under the Department of Education was authorized in the No Child Left Behind Act but has not yet been funded. The program is designed to promote schoolwide mental health strategies, provide training to elementary school and secondary school personnel to recognize early warning signs of mental illness, and increase student access to high-quality mental health services.

- STEPS to Healthier United States: Grants will be awarded to local and state health agencies and tribal entities that develop community action plans that focus on community and school interventions for both the specific diseases and related risk factors. These programs should target obesity, diabetes, asthma, heart disease, stroke, and cancer.

- Tobacco Cessation Activities at CDC: These funds are intended to expand the capacity of all state and local health departments, education agencies, and national organizations to build comprehensive tobacco control programs and develop a national public education campaign to reduce the appeal of tobacco products among young people.

PE4life Corporate Partners

Visit the PE4life Web site at www.pe4life.org to view a complete list of corporate sponsors who support the PE4life organization.

PE4life Academies

Naperville PE4life Academy

Phil Lawler, Academy Director
  Madison Jr. High School
  1000 River Oak
  Naperville, IL 60565
Paul Zientarski
  Naperville Central High School
  440 W. Aurora Avenue
  Naperville, IL 60540

Titusville PE4life Academy

Tim McCord, Academy Director
  Titusville School District
  415 Water Street
  Titusville, PA 16354

Grundy Center PE4life Academy

Rick Schupbach, Academy Co-Director

Beth Kirkpatrick, Academy Co-Director
  Grundy Center Elementary
  903 9th Street
  Grundy Center, IA 50638

PE4life is growing! Log onto the PE4life Web site, www.pe4life.org, for new PE4life Academies.

PE4life Headquarters

810 Baltimore Avenue, Suite 100
Kansas City, MO 64105
816-472-7345 (phone)
816-474-7329 (fax)
www.pe4life.org

PE4life Staff

Anne Flannery, President and CEO
Brenda VanLengen, VP, Operations
Phil Lawler, Director of Training and Outreach; PE4life Academy Director (Naperville, IL)
Carrie Gibson, Academy Coordinator
Kim Cairns, Office Manager

Sample Student Physical Education Pledge

The following is an example of a pledge that students can use to commit themselves to being dedicated to physical education.

PE4life: Proven Solutions That Inspire Active and Healthy Lifestyles

Madison Junior High School, Naperville, Illinois

Student Pledge

I pledge to do my best and participate in daily physical education.

I will use these skills to improve my physical and emotional health.

I will encourage others to enjoy and get involved with physical education.

I will ask my parents to get involved with my fitness and support me in these efforts.

I will also try hard to reach my potential and have fun.

I know physical activity can help strengthen my mind and body.

I will promote daily physical activity to my friends and family.

Sample Lesson Plans and Activities

In this appendix, you will find various samples of activities and lesson plans that help illustrate ideas from the book. For a quick glance, here are the sources where these materials originated:

The movement forms categories comes from Howe Academy, PE4life Wellness Education, Indianapolis, Indiana.

The sample of a one-week unit on cooperative education also comes from Howe Academy.

The cup-stacking unit was contributed by Rick Schupbach, co-director, PE4life Academy, Grundy Center, Iowa.

The Bounce at the Bell lesson plan is from *Building Strong Bones & Muscles* (Fishburne, 2005).

The At Least 10 Alligators lesson plan is from *Physical Best Activity Guide: Elementary Level Second Edition* (NASPE, 2005a).

Sports Roundup is also from *Physical Best Activity Guide: Elementary Level Second Edition* (NASPE, 2005a).

Fitting in Fitness is from *Physical Best Activity Guide: Middle and High School Levels Second Edition* (NASPE, 2005b).

The Evaluating Health Products lesson plan is also from *Physical Best Activity Guide: Middle and High School* (NASPE, 2005b).

Bridge Over the Raging River is from *Team Building Through Physical Challenges* (Glover & Midura, 1992).

Indiana's chalLenge is also from *Essentials of Team Building: Principles and Practices* (Midura & Glover, 2005).

The assessment of stages of motor skill development is from *Building Strong Bones & Muscles* (Fishburne, 2005).

The bench press technique activity is from *Physical Education for Lifelong Fitness: The Physical Best Teacher's Guide Second Edition* (NASPE, 2005c).

And the following forms are all from *It's Not Just Gym Anymore: Teaching Secondary School Students How to Be Active for Life* (McCracken, 2001):

Passing self-evaluation

Volleyball self-evaluation

Volleyball serve self-evaluation

Cyber spike

Dimensions of volleyball

Muscle matching

Cyber iron

Howe Academy
PE4life Wellness Education
Movement Forms Categories

We teach by categories, and we teach many topics within each category. That way, each student gets a variety. The teachers who like to teach only team sports must branch out with this grouping.

Fitness evaluation
Fitnessgram

Cooperative games
Character-building activities
Project Adventure
Classroom games

Individual activities
Tumbling
Track and field
Juggling
Fishing
Cup stacking
Skating
Biking
Hula hoops

Rhythmic
Line dance
Social dance
Folk dance
Tinikling

Enrichment
Games from other countries
Folk dance festival
Jump rope, hoops for heart
Journaling

Fitness activities
Yoga
Pilates
Step aerobics
Jump rope
Stretching
Resistance training
Sit-ups and push-ups
Isometrics
Tai chi
Circuit training
Scooters
Plyometrics
Interval training

Net games
Badminton
Pickleball
Volleyball
Tennis

Goal activities
Basketball
Soccer
Ultimate
Floor hockey
Team handball
Tswagway
Flag football
Rugby

Target activities
Bowling
Golf
Handball
Ring toss
Four square

Striking
Kickball
Softball
Wiffleball
Tetherball

Used with permission of Audrey Satterblom, Howe Academy, Indianapolis, IN.

Example of a One-Week Unit on Cooperative Education From Howe Academy

Day of week	Standards	Words	Engagement activities	Character goals	Assessment
Monday notes:	5, 6, 7	Lifetime sport Sportsmanship Procedure Personal space Personal challenge	Line up by height. Line up by birth month. Number of brothers and sisters, total. Ball and bounce to groups of eight, learning names—count off first to mix groups.	Say "thank you" four times. Say "you're welcome" four times. Say something nice to another twice. Goal: getting to know each other	Self-assessment—did I cooperate with others to make our group better? 1—I could do better. 2—I did OK. 3—I was terrific.
Tuesday notes:	5, 6, 7	Lifetime sport Sportsmanship Procedure Personal space Personal challenge	All Aboard—create an island and get everyone on the island. Alter—everyone on team goes to the opposite sides of the river by lily pads. No one can cross completely until everyone is on a lily pad.	Say "thank you" four times. Say "you're welcome" four times. Say something nice to another twice. Goal: teamwork	Self-assessment—did I cooperate with others to make our group better? 1—I could do better. 2—I did OK. 3—I was terrific.
Wednesday notes:	5, 6, 7	Lifetime sport Sportsmanship Procedure Personal space Personal challenge	Amoeba Electric Fence—height of 18 inches (46 centimeters) and bar over—all team members must help each other get to the other side.	Goal: trust and caring	Self-assessment—did I cooperate with others to make our group better? 1—I could do better. 2—I did OK. 3—I was terrific.
Thursday notes:	5, 6, 7	Lifetime sport Sportsmanship Procedure Personal space Personal challenge	Baton pass—with the tall tubes standing on the ends. Each person stands in a circle. The baton is in front of them on the end. When someone says, "Go," each person passes the baton to the right.	Goal: citizenship	Self-assessment—did I cooperate with others to make our group better? 1—I could do better. 2—I did OK. 3—I was terrific.
Friday notes:					Pedometers—1,500 steps

Used with permission of Audrey Satterblom, Howe Academy, Indianapolis, IN.

From *PE4life: Developing and Promoting Quality Physical Education*, by PE4life, 2007, Champaign, IL: Human Kinetics.

Cup-Stacking Unit

Pretest: With no instruction, test students on cup stacking a series of 3-6-3. With the use of the timer mats, students have three chances to complete the series, recording the times after each completion.

Day 1: Introduction and video (*Cup Stacking With Speed Stacks: See It, Believe It, Teach It! An Introduction to the Sport of Speed Stacking*)

- Watch the 3 stack, practice; 3-3-3 stack, practice; 6 stack, practice; 6-6 stack, practice; and then the 10 stack if time is available and when students are ready.
- Students learn the proper way to use the cup stacks and have time to practice the skills of cup stacking either on an ideal surface area or by using the timer mats.

Equipment: Video and VCR. One set of cup stacks per person. One timer mat per person.

Day 2: Introduction and progression activities

- Three-cup shuffle. Students work on handling the cups with a soft touch. They must hold three cups in one hand and drop one cup at a time into the opposite hand. Students try this with both hands.
- Cup stacking with three cups. Students work on up and down stacking with three cups, concentrating on using both hands.
- Cup stacking with two sets of three. Students must up stack and then down stack two sets of three stacks.
- Cup stacking with six cups. Students work on up stacking and down stacking one set of six cups.
- Students work on up stacking and down stacking a set of 3-6-3 (3-6-3 is timed by using the timer mats).

Equipment: One set of cups per person. One timer mat per person.

Day 3: Energized cup stacking: Speed stacking 500

- Students work in groups of two or three. One student up stacks and down stacks a set of 3-6-3, runs one lap around cones, and stops the timer. The other student goes next, trying to beat the time of his or her partner. They do this a couple of times, with students trying to beat each other's time as well as their own time.
- Students work in groups of two or three. One partner acts as a pit crew member and stands out of the way of her or his partner, who is the racer. The pit crew member directs the racer in performing the activity. The job of the racer is to up stack a set of three and then run around a set of cones back to the cups. The racer then up stacks a set of six and runs, up stacks a set of three and runs, down stacks a set of three and runs, down stacks a set of six and runs, down stacks a set of three, and then hits the timer! After all racers have completed the race, their partners become the racers. They begin when the teacher directs them to go.

Class discussion: Talk about lactic acid build-up. Explain why the time of their laps may not be as fast as they run more laps.

- In groups of two or three, students decide who will be the up stacker and who will be the down stacker. The up stacker up stacks a set of 3-6-3 and then runs around a set of cones. After arriving back at the cups, the up stacker gives his or her partner a high five, which serves as the cue to the partner to down stack the cups and take the lap around the cones. Each student does this twice. When the down stacker has run his or her second lap, he or she touches the timer to stop the time. Switch jobs so that everyone has a chance to play both roles.

- In groups of two or three, one student uses only the right hand and the other student uses the opposite hand. (Students may place the hand that they are not using behind their backs to ensure that they don't use it.) Students work together to up stack and then down stack a set of 3-6-3. Students then take one lap around the cones. Students must wait for their partners to arrive back at the cups before they can begin up stacking again. Students perform this activity twice, stopping the timer when both students have arrived back at the cups after their second lap.

- Cool-down: Students practice up and down stacking in a stationary position. Students may choose to do this individually or with a partner.

Equipment: For each group of two, a set of cup stacks, a timer mat, and one cone. Four large cones.

Day 4: Two activities

Activity 1: Face-Off

Students pair up with four stacks of six spread out about 2 feet (60 centimeters) apart. They begin with all the cups in an up stack position. Students begin facing each other on either side of the cup stacks. One partner is the up stacker, and the other is the down stacker. The down stacker begins. The up stacker immediately follows, up stacking all the cups. The down stacker goes back down and down stacks the cups again, trying to catch up with the up stacker. If the down stacker catches the up stacker, he or she wins. If the up stacker is able to up stack all the cups before the down stacker catches him or her, the up stacker becomes the winner. The students change roles after every round.

Activity 2: Team Build-Up

A set of two or three six-cup stacks per person is needed, as well as one timer mat for the entire class.

This activity challenges the class to see how quickly they can accomplish the task. One student, the leader, starts at the timer mat and lifts her or his hands to start the timer. The leader yells, "Go," which instructs the other students to begin up stacking all the cups out on the gym floor. When all the cups are up stacked, the students yell, "Go," instructing the leader, at the mat, to up stack those cups. When those cups are up stacked, the leader yells, "Go," cueing the other students to begin down stacking. When all the cups are down stacked, the students yell, "Go." The leader down stacks her or his stack and presses the timer to stop the time. Rotate the leader and see whether the class can beat their time in the previous round.

Variation: All students begin in the exterior portion of the playing area. When the leader yells, "Go," the students must run out and up stack at least three stacks. When they complete three stacks they run back to the outside, cueing the leader to begin his or her up stack. Enough cup stacks must be available for each student to have three stacks of six. (The leader may also participate, helping to up stack and down stack the cups in the middle of the floor.)

Day 5: Speed stack school challenge

- Each student has an opportunity to compete in the speed stack school challenge.
- Each student is timed using the timer mats.
- Each student performs the 3-3-3 and records the best time out of three trials.

(continued)

(continued)

- Each student performs the 6-6 and records the best time out of three trials.
- The two students with the fastest times in each class move on to the championship (see Culminating Activity on page 125).

Equipment: Four timer mats, 12 cups for each student, tables or mats for speed-stacking timed area.

Day 6: Speed stack school challenge (continued)

Each student performs the 6-6 and records the best time out of three trials.

Video and Cycle Stack

- Watch the video on the cycle stack (3-6-3, 6-6, 1-10-1, 3-6-3).
- Demonstrate the cycle.
- Students practice the cycle.

Equipment: Four timer mats, 12 cups for each student, tables or mats for speed-stacking timed area, speed-stacking video.

Day 7: Speed stack school challenge (continued)

- Students practice the cycle stack
- Each student performs the cycle stack and records the best time out of three trials.

Equipment: Four timer mats, 12 cups for each student, tables or mats for speed-stacking timed area.

Day 8: Culminating Game Activities

Activity 1: Builders and Bulldozers

- Divide students into two teams.
- Cups are spread out evenly on each side of the gym floor.
- Each team starts on one side of the gym floor.
- The object is for the team to cross the center line, down stack the opposing team's cups, run the cups back to the other side, and up stack the cups.
- The team with the most up stacked cups at the end of the game wins.
- For a variation, have students perform the activity while on scooters.

Activity 2: Super Cycle Circuit

- Students pair up.
- Cups are lined up in a row, set up in a 3-6-3, 6-6, 1-10-1 pattern for each group of two.
- One partner begins at the end with the 3-6-3 stack, while the other partner is at the other end with the 1-10-1.
- Partner 1 begins up stacking the 3-6-3, 6-6, and 1-10-1, and then gives a high five to partner 2.
- The high five sends partner 2 to down stack the 1-10-1, 6-6, and 3-6-3.
- Partner 2 touches the end line and runs down the line, up stacking the 3-6-3, 6-6, and 1-10-1.
- Partner 2 high fives partner 1, sending her or him down stacking the 1-10-1, 6-6, and 3-6-3.
- The team completes the cycle when partner 1 reaches the location where she or he started.

Culminating Activity: School speed stack championships
- The two finalists in each class compete in the championship finals a week after completion of the speed-stacking unit.
- Finals are held during the lunch period.
- The finalists for the 3-3-3 compete the first day, followed by the 6-6 finalists on the second day, the 3-6-3 finalists on the third day, and the cycle finalists on the last day.
- Begin with the students who come into the finals with the slowest times.
- Students compete in front of the school with the timer mats and a large stop clock.
- The format is single elimination.
- The student with the best time for each stack is crowned as school champion.
- Present certificates to the class finalists and the school champions.

Posttest: Retest the ability of students to stack a series of 3-6-3. Record the times of three trials. With no instruction, test the students on cup stacking a series of 3-6-3. With the use of the timer mats, students have three chances to complete the series, recording the time after each completion.

Reprinted by permission of Rick Schupbach.

From *PE4life: Developing and Promoting Quality Physical Education,* by PE4life, 2007, Champaign, IL: Human Kinetics.

BOUNCE AT THE BELL

Objectives

To build strong bones and muscles

Equipment Needed

None

Instructions

What is Bounce at the Bell?

Bounce at the Bell is a physical activity program in which children do a series of daily jumps to enhance their bone strength.

Why should my class participate in Bounce at the Bell?

The Bounce at the Bell program is designed to help children build strong bones during their formative years and thus reduce the risk of osteoporosis bone fractures later in life. Children who participated in a Bounce at the Bell program over an eight-month period demonstrated enhanced bone health compared with children who did not participate. In British Columbia, Canada, 8- to 10-year-old children who participated in a Bounce at the Bell program over an eight-month period significantly increased bone mass compared to children of similar ages who attended schools that did not participate in the program. Bounce at the Bell is now an integral part of the Action Schools! BC initiative (www.actionschools.bc.ca), which is ongoing and has shown the positive benefits of physical activity for bone health and academic performance (McKay, Tsang, Heinonen, MacKelvie, Sanderson, & Khan, 2005).

When should my class bounce?

You can jump in the morning, during recess, or over lunch—there is no one best time. Many instructors opt to make a class jumping schedule to match their teaching schedule.

How many times should children bounce per session?

Children begin with 5 jumps, 3 times a day, 4 days a week. Each month they add another jump to each jumping session, so in their eighth month they reach 36 jumps per day.

What types of jumps should my class be doing?

Jumping Jack Flash, Leaping Lizards, Terrific Triathletes, and Disco Dancers, all described in chapter 1, are the four best jumps for most children to perform during Bounce at the Bell. Activity cards for these jumps can be found on pages 128 and 129. As a class, you can decide which of the four jumps to perform. Children need not vary their jumps if they choose not to. If they enjoy Leaping Lizards the most, they can perform this jump every time.

If your students are doing single-leg landings (Disco Dancer and Terrific Triathlete), then the number of jumps needs to be doubled to achieve the correct total of landings per leg. The chart on the next page indicates the progression of jumping for an

Month	Number of two-foot landing jumps at each bell (Jumping Jack Flash or Leaping Lizards)	Number of one-foot landing jumps at each bell (Terrific Triathletes or Disco Dancers)	Number of jumping sessions per day	Total number of jumps per day
October	5	10 (5 per leg)	3	15
November	6	12 (6 per leg)	3	18
December	7	14 (7 per leg)	3	21
January	8	16 (8 per leg)	3	24
February	9	18 (9 per leg)	3	27
March	10	20 (10 per leg)	3	30
April	11	22 (11 per leg)	3	33
May	12	24 (12 per leg)	3	36

eight-month time frame. (Note this example begins in October, but start and finish times can be adjusted to fit personal schedules.)

Remember that children should jump 5 times, 3 times a day, 4 times a week and add 1 jump each month, according to the chart.

Safety Considerations

▷ Ensure each child has enough space to perform the jumps safely.

▷ Remove all sharp and hard objects and equipment from the jumping and bouncing area.

▷ Do not allow children to jump or bounce close to desks or other furniture.

Variations

▷ The example shown in the chart is for children at developmental levels 2 and 3. Bounce at the Bell can also be used with developmental level 1 children, but the number of bounces (jumps) required should be reduced for these children. In general, younger children tire more quickly than older children, but they also recover more quickly, so they should do fewer jumps with less rest time between them.

▷ To accommodate differences in fitness levels, developmental levels, and general individual differences, use personal task cards to determine the most appropriate number of bounces.

▷ Use journals or personal activity log books for goal setting and to record student performances.

▷ For a cross-curricular approach, use Bounce at the Bell in science when discussing force, Newton's laws of action and reaction, and how the body works. You can also discuss in health class or a health unit in another class the benefits of performing Bounce at the Bell.

Assessment

▷ Watch for proper form in jumping.

▷ Ask students to name the health benefits associated with Bounce at the Bell.

▷ Record performances in journals and personal activity log books and compare to goals set on task cards.

LEAPING LIZARDS

Equipment

None

Starting Position

- Stand with legs together and hands at sides.

Action

- Jump into a tuck position.
- Land in a scissors step with legs bent.

DISCO DANCERS

Equipment

None

Starting Position

- Stand with one leg up and bent.

Action

- Jump from the leg on the floor to the other leg.
- Repeat with the other leg.
- Try to get as much height as possible on each jump.

TERRIFIC TRIATHLETES

Equipment

None

Starting Position

- Stand with feet shoulder-width apart.

Action

- Jump from side to side with full power.
- Swing arms, skating style.

JUMPING JACK FLASH

Equipment

None

Starting Position

- Stand with feet together.

Action

- Jump up high.
- Spread legs wide to land.
- Bring hands over head and clap.

Reprinted, by permission, from G. Fishburne, H. McKay and S. Berg, 2005, *Building strong bones & muscles* (Champaign, IL: Human Kinetics), 126-129.

From *PE4life: Developing and Promoting Quality Physical Education,* by PE4life, 2007, Champaign, IL: Human Kinetics.

5.9 At Least 10 Alligators

PRIMARY LEVEL

Time is how long you need to hold a stretch to improve or maintain flexibility. Experts recommend that you hold each stretch, without bouncing or jerking, for 10 seconds (progressing to 30 seconds).

PURPOSE

Students will demonstrate an understanding that to stretch safely they must not bounce and that to improve or maintain flexibility they must hold stretches for 10 seconds or longer.

RELATIONSHIP TO NATIONAL STANDARDS

Physical Education Standard 4: The student achieves and maintains a health-enhancing level of physical fitness.

Health Education Standard 1: The student will comprehend concepts related to health promotion and disease prevention.

EQUIPMENT

None

PROCEDURE

1. Instruct students about the importance of not bouncing or jerking as they perform each stretch. Remind students that everyone has a different level of flexibility and

Reproducibles

- At Least 10 Alligators Sign
- At Least 10 Alligators Stretch Cards
- Stretching Reminders

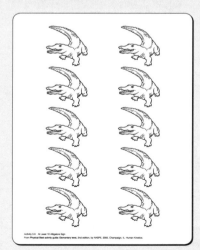

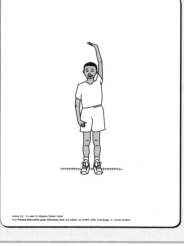

Stretching Reminders

1. **Never bounce when stretching**
2. **Never hold your breath when stretching. Inhale and exhale.**
3. **Never lock your joints when stretching.**
4. **Don't extend your joints too far when stretching.**
5. **Always hold the stretch for 10 to 30 seconds.**
6. **The stretch should never hurt.**
7. **Don't pull on your joints.**

that they should not compare their bodies to the bodies of other. They should not stretch to a point of undue discomfort. Tell them that today they will practice holding stretches for at least 10 seconds.

2. On your signal, students move in an activity area using a locomotor skill.

3. On the signal "Stop!" students freeze and ask you, "What do you see?" As you show the sign they respond, "At least 10 alligators."

4. Immediately after they say, "At least 10 alligators," you assume a stretch position of your choice, or hold up one of the "At Least 10 Alligators" Stretch Cards for a specific group of muscles. Then the students take the position. You cue the students to count the alligators by saying, "One alligator, two alligators, three alligators . . ." until they reach 10.

5. Repeat the activity by choosing another locomotor pattern, calling, "Stop," and ask, "What do you see?" They respond the same way by saying, "One alligator . . ."

TEACHING HINTS

- Monitor students closely to ensure that they do not bounce or jerk when stretching. Invite students who are stretching correctly to demonstrate for others.

- Create a bulletin board depicting pictures of various stretch poses. The title of the board could be "At Least 10 Alligators," and numbers 1 through 10 could connect the pictures.

- Explain to students that the first T in FITT stands for time. Remind them to hold stretching activities for at least 10 seconds, gradually working up to 30 seconds. Turn the first T on the FITT bulletin board into "Time = How Long!" Place a clock on the bulletin board next to the T for time.

SAMPLE INCLUSION TIP

Allow students to vary the locomotor and modify the stretch as needed. Use peer assistance when possible.

ASSESSMENT

- Ask students how long they should hold a stretch position.
- Have students demonstrate other stretches. Each stretch should last for at least 10 seconds and be free of bouncing and jerking.

Reprinted, by permission, from NASPE, 2004, *Physical best activity guide: Elementary level,* 2nd ed. (Champaign, IL: Human Kinetics), 120-121.

From *PE4life: Developing and Promoting Quality Physical Education,* by PE4life, 2007, Champaign, IL: Human Kinetics.

4.4

Sport Roundup

INTERMEDIATE LEVEL

Health benefits—Strong muscles allow us to participate in a variety of activities, including chores, work, play, and sports. Muscles that have good endurance allow us to work or play safely for long periods. In addition to having the benefit of playing and working harder and longer, good muscular strength and endurance can have many other benefits, including stronger bones, a stronger heart, good posture, and injury prevention.

PURPOSE

- Students will understand the health benefits associated with muscular strength and endurance.
- Students will identify connections between specific activities and muscular fitness.
- Students will participate in physical activities that help develop muscular fitness through specific physical activities.

RELATIONSHIP TO NATIONAL STANDARDS

Physical Education Standard 4: The student achieves and maintains a health-enhancing level of physical fitness.

Health Education Standard 1: The student will comprehend concepts related to health promotion and disease prevention.

Health Education Standard 3: The student will demonstrate the ability to practice health-enhancing behaviors and reduce health risks.

Reproducibles

- Sport Roundup Station Signs
- Health Benefit Signs
- Sport Roundup Task Sheet

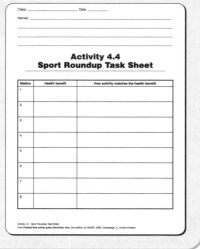

EQUIPMENT

- Energetic, upbeat music
- Clipboards and pencils (one per group)
- Jump ropes
- Low hurdles or small cones
- Ball, stick, puck, and so on, needed to practice goal scoring for any sport

---

Sample Station Ideas

1. Jump Rope Fun

Students jump rope, using multiple repetitions and sets to develop leg strength and endurance. Health benefit—stronger heart

2. Hurdler Leap

Students leap over a series of low obstacles on the ground, such as low hurdles or small cones, to improve leg strength. Health benefit—stronger bones

3. Score That Goal

Students take several shots on goal in a row (any sport). Health benefit—perform better

4. Kick Boxing

Students perform a variety of kicks and punches to develop upper body and lower body strength and endurance. Health benefit—stronger muscles

5. Strike Out

Students practice throwing form. Health benefit—prevents injury

6. Core Moves

From the pike position—clap hands together and then touch them to the floor repeatedly. From the pelvic raise position—alternately lift the right and left leg. Health benefit—good posture

7. Skating

Students pretend to skate in a pattern between and around cones, keeping the legs low to work the leg muscles. Health benefit—play and work longer

8. Line Dance

Have students perform a basic line dance routine, or other dance moves (such as those used in the activities You Should Be Dancing or Healthy Heart Hoe-Down from the aerobic fitness chapter). Health benefit—more energy

---

PROCEDURE

1. Using the eight Sport Round Up Station Signs or the Health Benefit Signs (provided on the CD-ROM), set up the stations around the activity space. Place the station activity and corresponding Health Benefit Signs side by side at each station. You may also create your own station signs for various sports and lifetime activities that interest your students.

(continued)

(continued)

2. Briefly review with the class, the definitions of muscular strength and muscular endurance. Also discuss the health benefits often associated with good muscular strength and endurance.

3. Divide students into small groups of four to six. Assign each group to a station.

4. Start music to signal students to perform the activity at that station. Stop the music to signal groups to stop and fill in their task sheet for that station. They should write in the health benefit that corresponds with the activity and a brief explanation of how the activity relates to the health benefit (for example, jumping rope works the leg muscles but also increases the heart rate, working the heart and making it stronger).

5. Start music again to signal students to proceed to the next station, and continue through the stations or until you have reached a predetermined time.

6. Discuss the task sheets as a group.

© Human Kinetics

TEACHING HINTS

▓ Make sure the activity stations are equal in time. Use a stopwatch or segmented or interval music to ensure consistent timing.

▓ To promote critical thinking, as a variation for older students, scatter the health benefit signs in the center of the activity space, and after performing the station, have students look through the health benefits and select one that matches their activity, and fill that in along with the explanation of their choice on their task card.

SAMPLE INCLUSION TIPS

Modifications to each activity:

▓ Jump rope—jumping over lines, secured hula hoop, or rope

▓ Hurdle—change the height of the hurdle

▓ Scoring—change the size of the puck, use a handled hockey stick, add color to the goal

▓ Kick boxing—have students perform a sitting curl-up in a wheelchair, add weight if needed by using a medicine ball

▓ Strike out—change the size and weight of the ball, use yarn ball or bean bags

▓ Skating—student in wheelchair can move in a pattern between and around cones.

When changing stations, use visual cues, such as red and green flags, for students with hearing impairments.

ASSESSMENT

▓ Collect task sheets after first asking students to identify which health benefit(s) are most important to them, and to write an answer on their task sheets.

▓ Have groups create their own station to improve muscular strength and endurance, and explain why they chose that activity, how it relates to muscular strength and endurance of that particular sport/activity, and what health benefits may be associated with that activity.

Reprinted, by permission, from NASPE, 2004, *Physical best activity guide: Elementary level,* 2nd ed. (Champaign, IL: Human Kinetics), 72-74.

From *PE4life: Developing and Promoting Quality Physical Education,* by PE4life, 2007, Champaign, IL: Human Kinetics.

3.6 Fitting in Fitness

MIDDLE SCHOOL

Frequency describes how often a person performs the targeted health-related physical activity. The minimum frequency for aerobic fitness activities is three days per week, while five to seven days is optimal.

PURPOSE

- Students will understand the importance of staying active most days of the week and will be encouraged to track their activity levels.
- Students will recognize physical activities that are aerobic (with oxygen) and anaerobic (without oxygen).
- Students will identify strategies that facilitate an active lifestyle.

RELATIONSHIP TO NATIONAL STANDARDS

Physical Education Standard 1: Demonstrates competency in motor skills and movement patterns needed to perform a variety of physical activities.

Physical Education Standard 3: Participates regularly in physical activity.

Physical Education Standard 4: Achieves and maintains a health-enhancing level of physical fitness.

Health Education Standard 1: Students will comprehend concepts related to health promotion and disease prevention.

Health Education Standard 3: Students will demonstrate the ability to practice health-enhancing behaviors and reduce health risks.

EQUIPMENT

The activities that you choose and the space that you have will dictate the equipment needed. Following are some examples of equipment needed for some of the activities described in the procedure.

- 1 to 6 basketballs
- 1 to 3 footballs
- 1 to 6 volleyballs
- 4 to 6 tennis rackets and balls
- 4 to 6 steps (for step aerobics)
- 4 to 6 hockey sticks and 2 hockey pucks or balls
- Music and player

(continued)

(continued)

Reproducibles

Note: These Fitting in Fitness handouts are only a sampling of some of the activities students might like to participate in outside of class. You can design additional handouts tailored to your students' needs.

- Basketball Handout (shown here as example)
- Jogging Handout (shown here as example)
- Tennis Handout (shown here as example)
- Aerobics Handout
- Football Handout
- Volleyball Handout
- Skating Handout
- Hockey Handout

Basketball

My friends and family are aware of, respect, and help me preserve the time of day that I set aside for physical activity!

That time is _____

I know exactly where a basketball is and can get to it quickly.

That place is _____

I have a list of ball-handling drills that I can do on my own.

_____
_____
_____
_____
_____
_____
_____

I have a list of friends and their phone numbers so that I can get a game together quickly.

_____
_____
_____
_____

I know where there is a basketball hoop or courts that I can bike, drive, walk, skate, or be driven to.

My method of transportation is _____

I have a water bottle for warm weather and hat and gloves for cold weather.

These items are located _____

I have the appropriate clothes and footwear for playing basketball.

These items are located _____

Activity 3.6 Basketball Handout
From *Physical Best activity guide: Middle and high school levels*, 2nd edition, by NASPE, 2005, Champaign, IL: Human Kinetics.

Jogging

My friends and family are aware of, respect, and help me preserve the time of day that I set aside for physical activity!

That time is _____

I know exactly where my running shoes are and can get to them quickly.

That place is _____

I know exactly where my running clothes are and can get to them quickly.

That place is _____

I have mapped out some specific courses of different distances to run. My one mile course is

_____
_____

My two mile course is

_____
_____
_____
_____

I have a running partner and his or her phone number.

Name _____ Number _____

I have a water bottle for warm weather and hat and gloves for cold weather.

These items are located _____

Activity 3.6 Jogging Handout
From *Physical Best activity guide: Middle and high school levels*, 2nd edition, by NASPE, 2005, Champaign, IL: Human Kinetics.

Tennis

My friends and family are aware of, respect, and help me preserve the time of day that I set aside for physical activity!

That time is _____

I know exactly where my tennis racket and ball are and can get to them quickly.

That place is _____

I have a list of friends and their phone numbers so that I can get a game together quickly.

_____ _____
_____ _____
_____ _____
_____ _____

I know where there are tennis courts or a wall that I can bike, drive, walk, skate, or be driven to.

My method of transportation is _____

I have a water bottle for warm weather and hat and gloves for cold weather.

These items are located _____

I have the appropriate clothes and footwear for playing tennis.

These items are located _____

Activity 3.6 Tennis Handout
From *Physical Best activity guide: Middle and high school levels*, 2nd edition, by NASPE, 2005, Champaign, IL: Human Kinetics.

PROCEDURE

1. Set up seven stations indoors or outdoors that will help your students to participate in seven different activities (e.g., basketball, volleyball, jogging, walking, Frisbee, football, soccer, dance, hockey, or aerobic dance). Include activities that are more aerobic (moderate intensity) and more anaerobic (vigorous intensity) in nature. Set up stations that appeal to your students and that represent activities that they most enjoy participating in both in physical education class and outside of class. Number the stations 1 to 7.

2. Remind the class that the Surgeon General suggests people should participate in physical activity most days of the week. Remind them that the time they spend in an activity and the intensity of the workout can affect how often they exercise.

3. Explain to the class that aerobic activities are activities in which their muscles require oxygen to produce energy. Tell students that in aerobic activities, they are active for a long period of time and can tell that their heart and lungs are working. Walking, biking, and jogging down the soccer field are aerobic activities. Explain

that aerobic activities should be done on most or all days of the week. But there is also another type of activity that is good for you. Anaerobic activities often are done for very short periods of time and use muscles in a more intense way. Think of sprinting or lifting a weight. Anaerobic physical activity is done in short, fast bursts in which the heart cannot supply blood and oxygen as fast as muscles use it (Corbin 2004).

© Human Kinetics

4. Tell the students that the seven stations that they will be moving through represent the seven days of the week. Ask the students what some of the reasons might be for taking a day off (e.g., to let your body recover after more intense, anaerobic activity). Inform them that in this activity they will be reviewing strategies to help them to stay active on most days of the week.

5. Describe to the class what activity they will be doing at each station. Examples:

- Basketball—Students could play one-on-one, two-on-two, or three-on-three; depending on the number of students who are at a station. They could practice running lay-ups, dribble in and out of cones, side shuffle as they pass, practice ball-handling drills, and so forth.

- Jogging—Students could run in pairs on a designated path or anywhere in sight of the teacher.

- Volleyball—Students could play two-on-two, or they could practice sets, forearm passes (to themselves, in pairs, with the group, or against a wall), and vertical jumps.

6. Divide the class into pairs. Tell the pairs of students to go to a station. Each station should be limited to three pairs.

7. Start the music.

8. Allow students to participate in an activity at their stations until the music stops at a predetermined time. Students at more intense (anaerobic) stations may need to take active rests (such as marching in place).

9. When the music stops, students rotate to the next station and then stretch.

10. When the music starts again, students should begin the new activity.

TEACHING HINTS

■ By changing the activities at each station, you can reinforce the idea that there are many types of physical activities for students to choose from.

(continued)

(continued)

■ Use the sport-specific handouts (on the CD-ROM) to start your students thinking about the strategies for staying active outside of class. The handouts can be filled in for homework.

SAMPLE INCLUSION TIP

If you have students with physical disabilities, work with an adapted P.E. specialist to adapt activities for each station.

ASSESSMENT

■ Conduct a question-and-answer session. Ask questions such as the following: What makes an activity aerobic? What activities were aerobic? What makes an activity anaerobic? What activities were anaerobic? What activities would be the easiest to participate in outside of class? What strategies for staying active were the most important to you and why?

■ Have students track their activity levels. They can develop their own method to track their activity frequency, intensity, time, and type by creating logs on paper or by generating a graph or calendar on the computer. Students can also use the "Presidential Youth Active Lifestyle log" (www.presidentschallenge.org) or other online fitness logs available to youth.

Reprinted, by permission, from NASPE, 2004, *Physical best activity guide: Secondary level,* 2nd ed. (Champaign, IL: Human Kinetics), 120-121.

From *PE4life: Developing and Promoting Quality Physical Education,* by PE4life, 2007, Champaign, IL: Human Kinetics.

9.2 Evaluating Health Products

MIDDLE AND HIGH SCHOOL

CONCEPTS

▦ **Quackery**—A method of advertising or selling that uses false claims to lure people into buying products that are worthless or even harmful.

▦ **Self-motivated exercise**—Becoming more physically active due to a personal need or desire to do so.

OBJECTIVES

▦ Evaluate health-related and fitness-related facilities.

▦ Describe the proper clothing and equipment that you need for physical activity.

▦ Evaluate printed material, videos, and Internet resources related to health and fitness.

OPENER

Introduce the lesson by using one of the following ideas:

▦ For the entire class, ask students to provide examples of products and services marketed by the exercise and diet industry. Through guided discussion, ask whether these products are effective or not and why.

▦ In small groups, ask students to list criteria they would use to determine whether a product or service has merit.

▦ Provide small groups with photos of advertisements for products and services. In their small groups, the students red-flag buzzwords and marketing strategies that the ads use to help sell products.

Reproducibles

▦ Sense and Nonsense, one per student

The answers for Sense and Nonsense are: 1-N, 2-N, 3-N, 4-N, 5-S, 6-N, 7-N, 8-N, 9-S, 10-N, 11-N, 12-N, 13-S, 14-N, 15-N, 16-S, 17-N, 18-N, 19-N, 20-N, 21-S, 22-N, 23-N, 24-N, 25-S

▦ Evaluating Health and Fitness Information and Services, one per student

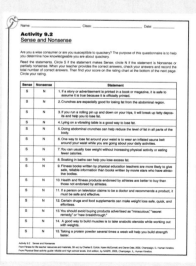

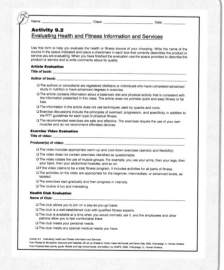

(continued)

(continued)

Photo by Dan Wendt

QUESTION OUTLINE TO GUIDE THE LESSON

1. What are the advantages of joining a fitness center or health club?
2. It is not necessary to join a health club in order to be active. What are some lower-cost alternatives to more expensive health clubs?
3. What are guidelines to keep in mind when considering joining a commercial health club?
4. Why should you make a trial visit to a health club you are considering joining?
5. What are some guidelines for selecting clothing and shoes for physical activity?
6. What types of exercise equipment are available to use in the home?
7. What do you need to consider if buying exercise equipment to use at home?
8. What guidelines should you consider when evaluating a book or article about exercise?
9. What guidelines should you consider when evaluating a book about nutrition and health?
10. What guidelines should you consider when evaluating the value of an exercise video?
11. How can you evaluate information on the Internet?
12. What are examples of reputable agencies and organizations for health, physical activity, and nutrition?

ENRICHMENT ACTIVITY: EXERCISE AT HOME

Objectives

Students will perform health-related fitness exercises using common household items. Students will learn that there is a wide variety of ways to exercise and that they do not have to pay a lot of money for equipment and programs advertised on television to get a good workout.

Equipment

The following equipment is needed for the stations described on the Exercising at Home Worksheet. You can modify the stations and worksheet as needed to fit your situation.

- Several small benches or steps, for stair stepping
- Bleachers (preferable) or several benches or steps, for step push-up
- Several towels, enough for use at four stations
- Several broomsticks, enough for use at four stations
- 20 or more food cans of various sizes, for use at two stations
- Several jump ropes
- CD player and music

Opener

1. Place a sign and equipment at each station.
2. Have students do a warm-up.
3. After the warm-up, hand out the Exercising at Home worksheet to each student.
4. Divide the class into five groups, one for each station. Assign each group a station.
5. Have the students divide equally among the different exercises at each station. Have students read the directions and then practice the assigned exercise.
6. One student from each exercise will demonstrate that exercise to the class.
7. Have each group return to their starting station and perform the assigned exercise.
8. On a signal, have groups rotate to the next station.
9. After all students have had a chance to use each of the five types of exercise "equipment," have students cool-down.

CLOSING DISCUSSION

Review the guidelines students should follow if choosing a health club to join. Ask students what they would evaluate on a trial visit to a health club. Review the wide variety of home exercise equipment available and highlight the advantages and disadvantages of home exercise. Review what to look for when evaluating books and articles, videos, and the Internet. Finally, provide Web sites of reputable associations for health, physical activity, and nutrition.

Reproducible

- Exercising at Home, 1 per student

Reprinted, by permission, from NASPE, 2004, *Physical best activity guide: Secondary level,* 2nd ed. (Champaign, IL: Human Kinetics), 181-183.

From *PE4life: Developing and Promoting Quality Physical Education,* by PE4life, 2007, Champaign, IL: Human Kinetics.

Bridge Over the Raging River

▷ Description

Bridge Over the Raging River is a terrific challenge that requires all group members to be integral parts of the solution as they cross a river using four automobile tires, two 8-foot-long (2.5-meter-long) boards, and two ropes. This challenge is not intellectually difficult, but most groups find it physically difficult. This challenge is one of the first we ever did.

Group members travel from one end of a space (land) to the other end without touching the floor (river). The length of a basketball court works well. The group must carry all equipment to the other side.

▷ Success Criteria

The group masters the task when all group members cross the river without breaking the rules and with their equipment.

▷ Equipment

- Four automobile tires (large tires are harder to use).
- Two 8-foot (2.5-meter) two-by-fours (boards about 3.8 centimeters thick and 9.0 centimeters wide).
- Two jump ropes as shown in figure 8.3. Eight- to 14-foot (2.5- to 4.3-meter) lengths of sash cord work best.

▷ Setup

Label distinct starting and ending lines and use a straight-line open area (the length of a gymnasium) free from any objects or walls.

The group creates a series of movable bridges using the two-by-fours to close the gaps between tires. Groups often use one tire as an island to stand on as group members transfer equipment forward. They tie the jump ropes to a tire or two-by-four to pull the equipment forward.

Remind participants that they must move the two-by-fours safely. They must be careful not to hit teammates accidentally with a board or to step on one end of a board so that it flips up.

▷ Rules and Sacrifices

1. Group members may not touch the river (floor).
2. A group member may not step on a two-by-four if it has one end in the river (the two-by-four may sag into and touch the river without penalty).
3. If a group member breaks a rule, the group must take the bridge back to the starting position and start over.
4. No one can use last names or put-downs.

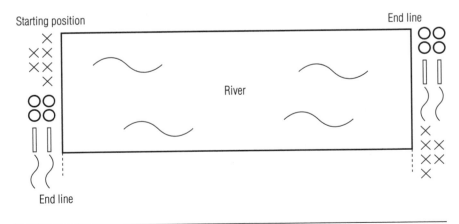

Figure 8.3 Starting and ending positions for Bridge Over the Raging River.

Possible Solutions

Most groups follow one basic pattern to solve this task. Groups make a movable bridge. As the group advances, it passes the tires and two-by-fours forward. Group members must share space on a tire.

Participants need good balance and must hold on to or physically assist teammates throughout the challenge. They have no choice but to help one another constantly! The group also needs to communicate how it intends to pass the equipment along. If someone tries to roll a tire to a teammate who is unaware of the plan, the tire may roll off course, causing an unwanted detour. Participants may attempt to move tires by getting their feet inside a tire and jumping along with it (hard to do but possible). Most groups attempting the challenge find it difficult to have several teammates balance on a tire at once. Multiple mistakes often occur, which generally means that the group must start the task over.

Conclusion of the Task

The group is successful when it crosses the river (the length of the gymnasium or basketball court) with all assigned equipment in its possession. You may institute a time limit, basing success on criteria other than crossing the river. When group members complete the challenge, have them take the equipment back to the starting position for the next group to use.

Additions and Variations

- Smaller tires, such as boat trailer tires of 11 to 12 inches (28 to 30 centimeters), create a crowded area and make it more difficult for several people to maintain good balance.
- You might place obstacles (cones, balance beams, parallel bars) in the river that the group must travel around, over, or under.
- Another variation is to have the group carry some object, such as a football blocking dummy, that represents an injured group member who must be rescued.

Safety Considerations

Participants need to move the two-by-fours carefully. They must not drop them, leave them standing on end, throw them, jerk them, or otherwise handle them recklessly. We have already mentioned that participants must avoid stepping on one end of a board if the other end is not supported. If a board were to flip up, if could hit someone, an especially painful event if a teammate is straddling the board with his or her feet. Teammates should not grab onto one another and cause one or both to fall off the bridge in a careless manner. This challenge includes a lot of lifting and moving of tires. Participants need to lift properly and safely.

Reprinted, by permission, from D. Glover and D.W. Midura, 1992, *Team building through physical challenges* (Champaign, IL: Human Kinetics), 52.

From *PE4life: Developing and Promoting Quality Physical Education,* by PE4life, 2007, Champaign, IL: Human Kinetics.

Indiana's Challenge DVD

▷ DESCRIPTION

ndiana's Challenge, created in one of our summer classes, has become one of our core challenges not only because of its clever design but also because it doesn't require much space and uses very little equipment. In addition, the challenge has multiple solutions.

Group members gather around a 10-foot (3-meter) diameter circle, such as the jump-ball circle of a basketball court. The challenge is to remove a basketball that is balanced on an 18-inch (45-centimeter) cone from the middle of the circle. Group members have jump ropes that they use to get the ball out of the circle. One element of the challenge is that the group must find three different ways to remove the ball. One of the three methods must include flinging the ball so that a group member can catch it in the air. Another element of the challenge is that the ball may not touch the floor either inside or outside the circle. In addition, no group member may step over the line or touch the inside of the circle with any body part. Whenever the ball falls to the floor, one group member may cross the line to place the ball onto the cone. While in the circle, this group member may not help manipulate any of the ropes.

▷ SUCCESS CRITERIA

The group completes the task when it invents three methods of removing the ball from the cone and getting it into the hands of a group member outside the circle. As stated previously, at least one method must include flinging the ball so that a group member catches it in the air. The group must use some combination of the ropes.

▷ EQUIPMENT

Provide a basketball and four jump ropes, approximately 10 to 12 feet (3.0 to 3.6 meters) long. We recommend sash cord rope.

▷ SETUP

Place the 18-inch (45-centimeter) cone on the center of the 10-foot (3-meter) circle. Make sure that the cone has an opening that will allow a basketball to rest on the top of it. Place the ropes outside the circle. If you do not have an existing circle in your facility, create one with chalk or vinyl tape. You could use another shape, but a circle adds an interesting dimension when the group tries to move around.

▷ RULES AND SACRIFICES

1. If the ball touches the floor, one group member may cross the circle line to replace the ball on the cone.
2. Participants may not cross the line at any time while trying to remove the ball.
3. The teammate replacing the ball on the cone may not manipulate the ropes while in the circle.
4. The ball may never touch the ground inside or outside of the circle.
5. No one may call others by their last names or use put-downs.
6. If a group member breaks a rule, the group must stop, replace the ball, and begin again.

▷ POSSIBLE SOLUTIONS

Almost every time we use this challenge, we see groups come up with new twists to solving it. One method is to cross the ropes so that two ropes are perpendicular to two other ropes. The group then creates a small cradle in which to rest the ball. Group members lift the ball and carry it out of the circle. They also use this method to lift the ball and fling it into the air so that a group member can catch it. In both cases, group members must hold the rope tight so that the ball does not slip through. Another method is to create a channel with the ropes. One side lifts its end of the ropes and rolls the ball to the other side of the circle, where a group member catches it. We have also seen a group place two ropes parallel to one another about 8 inches (20 centimeters) apart and then weave the other ropes back and forth to create a long, skinny net. The group uses this net to carry the ball out of the circle, roll the ball out of the circle, and fling the ball out of the circle.

▷ CONCLUSION OF THE TASK

The group completes the task when it creates three different methods of removing the ball from the cone. Group members should then replace the ball on the cone, untie any knots that they may have made, and place the equipment neatly outside the circle.

▷ ADDITIONS AND VARIATIONS

We have seen so many solutions to this task that we have not felt the need to create any variations.

▷ SAFETY CONSIDERATIONS

This challenge presents no obvious safety issues.

Reprinted, by permission, from D.W. Midura and D. Glover, 2005, *Essentials of team building: Principles and practices* (Champaign, IL: Human Kinetics), 118-119.

From *PE4life: Developing and Promoting Quality Physical Education,* by PE4life, 2007, Champaign, IL: Human Kinetics.

Assessment of Stages of Motor Skill Development

Assessing children's fundamental motor skills is an important component of the elementary school physical education program. Fundamental motor skills can be broken down into three developmental phases: initial, elementary, and mature patterns of movement. Ideally, by the end of adolescence, all children under typical circumstances should be performing fundamental motor skills at a mature pattern of movement. The following provides an easy-to-use developmental assessment checklist of the locomotion skills that help produce muscle and bone development in children.

	Initial Stage	**Elementary Stage**	**Mature Stage**
Hopping	☐ Very little balance. ☐ May only do one or two hops. ☐ Little height or distance. ☐ Body appears rigid.	☐ Balance is better but is still not under control. ☐ May only do a few hops. ☐ Arms move bilaterally and very quickly. ☐ There is a slight forward lean.	☐ Arms are used for force and not balance. ☐ Arms move together. ☐ Greater forward lean. ☐ The nonsupporting leg moves in time with other leg.
Jumping	☐ Arms do not start the jumping action. ☐ Little emphasis placed on the length of the jump. ☐ Both feet may not be used at the same time for takeoff or landing. ☐ Body may fall backward at landing.	☐ Arms begin jumping action. ☐ Arms are at the front of the body before jump. ☐ Arms are used for balance in the air. ☐ There is a bigger crouch prior to the jump.	☐ Arms are high and behind the body before the jump. ☐ Arms swing forward when jumping. ☐ More emphasis placed on distance. ☐ Weight of the body is forward at landing.
Leaping	☐ Gains very little height and distance. ☐ Arms are not used very much. ☐ The takeoff leg is inconsistently used.	☐ Arms are mainly used for balance. ☐ Little height off of the ground. ☐ Legs are still quite bent when off the ground.	☐ Relaxed, smooth flow. ☐ Takeoff leg is forceful. ☐ Legs are fully extended when off the ground.
Skipping	☐ Arms are used very little. ☐ Skips on one foot. ☐ Stepping action instead of skip.	☐ Landing appears to be heavy or flat footed. ☐ Arms are better used to aid in skip. ☐ Step and hop are coordinated.	☐ Whole body moves in a smooth flowing action. ☐ Little height on the hop. ☐ Landings are on the toes.

Bench Press Technique

Resistance used

40 to 50 percent of body weight

Starting position

Elbows are straight; feet are flat on the floor or flat on the end of bench or platform; buttocks and shoulders touch bench; back is not excessively arched; bar is over upper chest; bar is horizontal.

Points available: 0-6

Points earned: _____

Lowering (eccentric) phase

Descent of bar is controlled; elbows are out to side; forearms are perpendicular to the floor; bar touches chest at nipple level; there is no bounce on chest touch; bar is horizontal; feet stay flat on floor; back is not excessively arched; head stays still.

Points available: 0-7

Points earned: _____

Up (concentric) phase

Back is not excessively arched; elbows are out to sides; bar is horizontal; both arms straighten at same speed; motion is smooth and continuous; head stays still; feet stay flat on floor.

Points available: 0-9

Points earned: _____

Finishing position

Same position as starting position.

Points available: 0-3

Points earned: _____

Total points available: 0-25

Total points earned: _____

Technique tips

- Inhale as you lower the weight and exhale as you lift it.
- A spotter should be behind the lifter's head and should assist the lifter with getting the barbell into the starting position and returning the barbell to the rack when finished. Impress on young weight trainers the importance of a spotter during the exercise because the bar is pressed over the lifter's face, neck, and chest.
- Learn this exercise with an unloaded barbell or long stick.
- Do not bounce the barbell off the chest, and do not lift your buttocks off the bench during this exercise.
- Avoid hitting the upright supports by positioning your body about three inches from the supports before you start.

Reprinted, by permission, from W. Kraemer and S. Fleck, 1993, *Strength training for young athletes* (Champaign, IL: Human Kinetics), 30.

From *PE4life: Developing and Promoting Quality Physical Education,* by PE4life, 2007, Champaign, IL: Human Kinetics.

Passing Self-Evaluation

Name: _____ Date: _____

| **O** = not yet | **X** = getting better | **+** = proper technique |

Preparation phase

1st day	2nd day	3rd day	
1. _____	_____	_____	Move feet to ball
2. _____	_____	_____	Join hands
3. _____	_____	_____	Feet shoulder-width apart
4. _____	_____	_____	Knees bent, body low
5. _____	_____	_____	Form a platform with arms
6. _____	_____	_____	Thumbs parallel
7. _____	_____	_____	Elbows locked
8. _____	_____	_____	Arms parallel to thighs
9. _____	_____	_____	Back straight
10. _____	_____	_____	Eyes track ball

Execution phase

1st day	2nd day	3rd day	
1. _____	_____	_____	Receive ball in front of body
2. _____	_____	_____	Slight extension of legs
3. _____	_____	_____	No arm swing
4. _____	_____	_____	Transfer weight forward
5. _____	_____	_____	Contact ball away from body
6. _____	_____	_____	Slant platform toward target
7. _____	_____	_____	Hips move forward
8. _____	_____	_____	Watch ball contact arms

Follow-through phase

1st day	2nd day	3rd day	
1. _____	_____	_____	Keep hands joined
2. _____	_____	_____	Elbows remain locked
3. _____	_____	_____	Platform follows ball to target
4. _____	_____	_____	Keep arms below shoulder level
5. _____	_____	_____	Transfer weight forward
6. _____	_____	_____	Watch ball to target

Reprinted, by permission, from B. McCracken, 2001, *It's not just gym anymore* (Champaign, IL: Human Kinetics), 89.
From *PE4life: Developing and Promoting Quality Physical Education,* by PE4life, 2007, Champaign, IL: Human Kinetics.

Volleyball Setting Self-Evaluation

Name: _____ Date: _____

| **O** = not yet | **X** = getting better | **+** = proper technique |

Preparation phase

	1st day	2nd day	3rd day	
1.	_____	_____	_____	Move to ball
2.	_____	_____	_____	Establish position
3.	_____	_____	_____	Square shoulders to target
4.	_____	_____	_____	Feet in comfortable stride
5.	_____	_____	_____	Bend arms, legs, and hips
6.	_____	_____	_____	Hands above head
7.	_____	_____	_____	Hands in front of forehead
8.	_____	_____	_____	Look through hands
9.	_____	_____	_____	Follow ball to target

Execution phase

	1st day	2nd day	3rd day	
1.	_____	_____	_____	Contact ball on bottom
2.	_____	_____	_____	Contact ball on fingers
3.	_____	_____	_____	Extend arms and legs toward target
4.	_____	_____	_____	Transfer weight toward target
5.	_____	_____	_____	Direct ball to desired height
6.	_____	_____	_____	Direct ball to hitter's hand or toward sideline

Follow-through phase

	1st day	2nd day	3rd day	
1.	_____	_____	_____	Extend arms
2.	_____	_____	_____	Point hand toward target
3.	_____	_____	_____	Hips move toward target
4.	_____	_____	_____	Transfer weight toward target
5.	_____	_____	_____	Move in direction of set

Reprinted, by permission, from B. McCracken, 2001, *It's not just gym anymore* (Champaign, IL: Human Kinetics), 90.
From *PE4life: Developing and Promoting Quality Physical Education,* by PE4life, 2007, Champaign, IL: Human Kinetics.

Volleyball Serve Self-Evaluation

Name: _____   Date: _____

O = not yet	**X** = getting better	**+** = proper technique

Preparation phase

	1st day	2nd day	3rd day	
1.	_____	_____	_____	Feet comfortable
2.	_____	_____	_____	Weight even
3.	_____	_____	_____	Shoulders square
4.	_____	_____	_____	Ball at waist
5.	_____	_____	_____	Ball in front of body
6.	_____	_____	_____	Use open hand
7.	_____	_____	_____	Eyes on ball

Execution phase

	1st day	2nd day	3rd day	
1.	_____	_____	_____	Swing arm back
2.	_____	_____	_____	Weight to rear
3.	_____	_____	_____	Swing arm forward
4.	_____	_____	_____	Weight to front
5.	_____	_____	_____	Contact ball on heel of hand
6.	_____	_____	_____	Eyes on ball

Follow-through phase

	1st day	2nd day	3rd day	
1.	_____	_____	_____	Swing arm toward top of net
2.	_____	_____	_____	Weight to front foot
3.	_____	_____	_____	Move onto court

Reprinted, by permission, from B. McCracken, 2001, *It's not just gym anymore* (Champaign, IL: Human Kinetics), 91.
From *PE4life: Developing and Promoting Quality Physical Education,* by PE4life, 2007, Champaign, IL: Human Kinetics.

Cyber Spike

Name: _____   Date: _____

Go to **www.volleyball.org/general/index.html**.

1. List the four most important moves in volleyball.

2. How old is volleyball?

3. In what year was volleyball introduced at the Olympics?

4. What was the prize for the first two-man beach volleyball tournament?

5. Find a game at **www.volleyball.org/playing/index.html**.

Reprinted, by permission, from B. McCracken, 2001, *It's not just gym anymore* (Champaign, IL: Human Kinetics), 92.
From *PE4life: Developing and Promoting Quality Physical Education*, by PE4life, 2007, Champaign, IL: Human Kinetics.

Dimensions of Volleyball

Name: _____   Date: _____

1. What do you need to know to play volleyball? List at least five items in their order of importance.

2. What other activities have you done that are similar to volleyball? List five.

3. Choose one of the activities you listed above and tell how it is similar to volleyball.

4. Let's play. Make a plan to play volleyball (who, when, where, how).

5. Now that you have finished the unit, what did you learn?

Reprinted, by permission, from B. McCracken, 2001, *It's not just gym anymore* (Champaign, IL: Human Kinetics), 93.
From *PE4life: Developing and Promoting Quality Physical Education,* by PE4life, 2007, Champaign, IL: Human Kinetics.

Muscle Matching

Name: _____ *Date:* _____

Part I

List the muscles used for each of the following exercises:

Bench press	Biceps curl	Leg curl
T row	Triceps pushdown	Lunge
Military press	Squat	Calf raise
Lat pulldown	Leg extension	Crunch

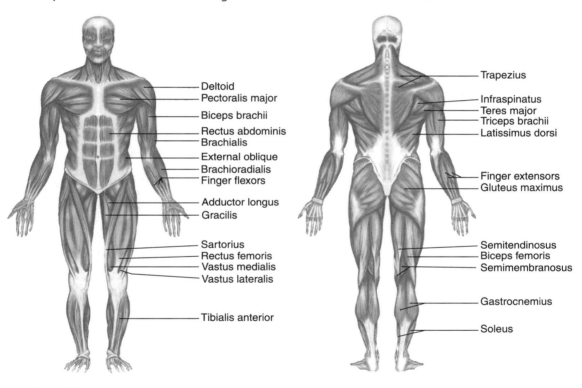

Part II

Antagonistic pairings: Draw a line connecting exercises that use antagonistic muscles.

Bench press	Triceps pushdown
Biceps curl	Lat pulldown
Military press	Leg curl
Leg extension	T row

Reprinted, by permission, from B. McCracken, 2001, *It's not just gym anymore* (Champaign, IL: Human Kinetics), 206.
From *PE4life: Developing and Promoting Quality Physical Education,* by PE4life, 2007, Champaign, IL: Human Kinetics.

Cyber Iron

Name: _____   Date: _____

Note: The Web addresses used in this form were accurate at the time of publication. If the site is no longer active, search **www.yahoo.com** or a similar search engine to find the answers.

1. These sites provide good advice about maintaining fitness: **www.justmove.org** and **www.fitnessonline.com.** What did you find interesting?

2. Surf the Web to find a workout for your sport. Describe the workout you found most interesting.

3. Go to this site: **www.fitnesslink.org** to find out how to create a home gym. Describe what you'd need to do to create a home gym. Is a home gym right for you?

4. Surf this site: **www.healthclubs.com** to find a health club near you.
   a. Where is the club located?

   b. How much does it cost to become a member?

   c. What is the phone number?

   d. What kinds of services and facilities does it have?

   e. How do you choose the right club for you?

5. Here is a good site to find other places: **http://k2.kirtland.cc.mi.us/ ~ balbachl/fitness.htm**

List some of the sites you found interesting and tell why.

Links to Physical Education Web Sites

Visit PE4life's Web site at www.pe4life.org for information about training at a PE4life Academy, receiving follow-up support for those who have trained at a PE4life Academy, finding various physical education resources, locating information on applying for grants, discovering PE4life corporate sponsors, and viewing links to the following organizations.

National Standards

www.aahperd.org/naspe/template.cfm?
template=publications-nationalstan-
dards.html

Government, Organization, and Association Sites

www.pe4life.org

www.aahperd.org

www.aahperd.org/naspe

www.cdc.gov

www.ncppa.org

www.americanheart.org

www.cancer.org

www.shapeup.org

www.welcoa.org

www.fitness.gov

www.teachphysed.com

www.obesity.org

www.isbe.net

http://sandiegocahperd.net

www.wahperd.org

www.iahperd.org

www.cahperd.org

www.tahperd.org

Resources and Programs

www.aahperd.org/naspe/physicalbest

www.HumanKinetics.com

www.fitnessgram.net

www.fitnessforlife.org

www.pecentral.org

www.pelinks4u.org

www.sparkpe.org

www.teachphysed.com

www.HumanKinetics.com/physicalbest

Equipment Companies

www.sportime.com

www.gophersport.com

www.flaghouse.com

www.bechoosy.org

Adventure Education

www.outdoored.com/default.aspx

www.wilderdom.com/oeresources/index.
htm

www.wilderdom.com/theories.htm

www.aeminfo.mb.ca/whyaem.html

http://webdb.iu.edu/hperweb/iole/index.
cfm

Other

www.shambles.net/pages/staff/pe__hft

www.eduwight.iow.gov.uk/curriculum/
post16/pe/useful_physical_educational_
websites

www.pecentral.org/websites/kidsites.html

http://people.bu.edu/judim/2005/07/
health-and-pe-websites.html

http://people.bu.edu/nj339/2005/07/pe-websites.html

http://pe.myteacher.dvusd.com/classwork

www.mrgym.com

www.actionbasedlearning.com/cgi-bin/index.pl

www.gymarchive.com

www.education.gov.ab.ca/physicaleducationonline

http://pe1.org

http://members.cox.net/pefun/index.shtml

http://schoolnotes.com/15656/gerc.html

www.actionbasedlearning.com/cgi-bin/index.pl

www.presidentschallenge.org/index.aspx

http://db.tomassetti.net/stridelengthto stepsconverter.aspx

http://db.tomassetti.net/thrhome.aspx

http://db.tomassetti.net/bmi_home.aspx

http://db.tomassetti.net/metscalculator.aspx

http://fitness1st.net/timer/index.htm

http://pe1.org/resources/graphicdown loads.htm

http://fit.pe1.org/

http://pe1.org/bushnell/index.htm

http://hpe441.pe1.org

www.isobelkleinman.com

http://pe1.org/fit1stpublic

http://pe.betances.us

http://pe1.org/presentations/using_web_forms_files/frame.htm

www.cdc.gov/youthcampaign

www.kidshealth.org

www.kidskonnect.com/PhysicalFitness/Fitness.html

References and Resources

References

Ardovino, L., & Sanders, S. (1997). The development of a physical education assessment report. *Teaching Elementary Physical Education, 8*(3), 23-25.

Corbin, C., & Lindsey, R. (2007). *Fitness for life* (updated 5th ed.). Champaign, IL: Human Kinetics.

Dale, D., & Corbin, C. (2000). Physical activity participation of high school graduates following exposure to conceptual or traditional physical education. *Research Quarterly for Exercise and Sport, 71*(1), 61-68.

Dale, D., Corbin, C., & Cuddihy, T. (1998). Can conceptual physical education promote physically active lifestyles? *Pediatric Exercise Science, 10*(2), 97-109.

Fishburne, G., McKay, H., & Berg, S. (2005). *Building strong bones & muscles*. Champaign, IL: Human Kinetics.

Gallahue, D., & Donnelly, F.C. (2003). *Developmental physical education for all children* (4th ed.). Champaign, IL: Human Kinetics.

Glover, D., & Anderson, L. (2003). *Character education–43 fitness activities for community building*. Champaign, IL: Human Kinetics.

Graham, G. (2001). *Teaching children physical education: Becoming a master teacher* (2nd ed.). Champaign, IL: Human Kinetics.

Hellison, D. (2003). *Teaching responsibility through physical activity*. Champaign, IL: Human Kinetics.

Hellison, D. (1985). *Goals and strategies for teaching physical education*. Champaign, IL: Human Kinetics.

Hichwa, J. (1998). *Right fielders are people too: An inclusive approach to teaching middle school physical education*. Champaign, IL: Human Kinetics.

Hopple, C. (2005). *Elementary physical education teaching & assessment: A practical guide* (2nd ed.). Champaign, IL: Human Kinetics.

Kelly, L., & Melograno, V. (2004). *Developing the physical education curriculum: An achievement-based approach*. Champaign, IL: Human Kinetics.

McCracken, B. (2001). *It's not just gym anymore: Teaching secondary school students how to be active for life*. Champaign, IL: Human Kinetics.

Melograno, V. (2006). *Professional and student portfolios for physical education* (2nd ed.). Champaign, IL: Human Kinetics.

Midura, D., & Glover, D. (2005). *Essentials of team building: Principles and practices*. Champaign, IL: Human Kinetics.

Morrow, J.R., Jr., & Freedson, P.S. (1994). Relationship between habitual physical activity and aerobic fitness in adolescents. *Pediatric Exercise Science, 6*, 315-329.

Morrow, J.R., Jr., Jackson, A.W., & Payne, V.G. (1999). Physical activity promotion and school physical education. *Research Digest, Series 3*(7), Washington, DC: President's Council on Physical Fitness and Sports.

Mosston, M., and Ashworth, S. (2002). *Teaching physical education* (5th ed.). San Francisco: Benjamin Cummings.

Mosston, M. and Ashworth, S. (1998). *Teaching physical education*. Columbus: Merrill.

National Association for Sport and Physical Education (NASPE). (2005a). *Physical Best activity guide: Elementary level* (2nd ed.). Champaign, IL: Human Kinetics.

National Association for Sport and Physical Education (NASPE). (2005b). *Physical Best activity guide: Middle and high school levels* (2nd ed.). Champaign, IL: Human Kinetics.

National Association for Sport and Physical Education (NASPE). (2005c). *Physical education for lifelong fitness: The Physical Best teacher's guide* (2nd ed.). Champaign, IL: Human Kinetics.

Silverman, S., & Ennis, C. (2003). *Student learning in physical education: Applying research to enhance instruction* (2nd ed.). Champaign, IL: Human Kinetics.

U.S. Department of Health and Human Services (USDHHS). (2000). *Healthy people 2010* (2nd ed.). Washington, DC: U.S. Government Printing Office.

Winnick. J.P., and Short, F.X. (1999). *The Brockport Physical Fitness Test manual.* Champaign, IL: Human Kinetics.

Resources

The following resource materials provide more information about building a quality physical education program.

Adventure Education Resources

www.outdoored.com/default.aspx
This is an excellent starting link for outdoor and adventure information for the professional.

www.wilderdom.com/oeresources/index.htm
A portal for organizations, research, and other information about adventure.

www.wilderdom.com/theories.htm
This site is a great place to go to for theories and research.

www.aeminfo.mb.ca/whyaem.html
This link provides good definitions, theories, overview, and so on.

http://webdb.iu.edu/hperweb/iole/index.cfm
The purpose of this site to help users search for journal articles about recreation and education.

Books

Jensen, C., and Guthrie, S. (2006). *Outdoor Recreation in America* (6th ed.). Champaign, IL: Human Kinetics. This resource now includes adventure information.

Priest, S., and Gass, M. (2005). *Effective Leadership in Adventure Programming* (2nd ed.). Champaign, IL: Human Kinetics. The first couple of chapters give an overview of adventure.

Project Adventure. (in press). *Adventure Education: Theory and Applications.*

Wagstaff and Attraim. (in press). *Adventure Technical Skills: A Curriculum Guide.* This resource has unit plans for instructors working with beginning level students.

Outside Resources

Boston Public Schools. See www.pa.org/press/pa_050513.pdf. Includes four-year research study on adventure with Project Adventure.

Gilbertson, K., Bates, T., McLaughlin, T., & Ewert, A. (2006). *Outdoor Education: Methods and Strategies.* Champaign, IL: Human Kinetics. Most lesson plans are appropriate for use in a physical education curriculum.

Hughes, J.D. (2003). *No Standing Around in My Gym.* Champaign, IL: Human Kinetics.

Illinois State Board of Education. At www.isbe.net you can find many samples of assessments and lesson plans, which are linked to state and national standards. Project Adventure. See www.pa.org/press/PA_050513.pdf

Pangrazi, R. (2004). *Dynamic Physical Education for Elementary School Children.* San Francisco: Pearson. (Any of Pangrazi's curriculum books and lesson plan books would be a good resource.)

Project Adventure. See www.pa.org/press/PA_050513.pdf

Video: *No More Dodgeball.* Developed by the Michigan AHPERD in 1996, this 27-minute video is a well-developed look at how physical education has changed.

About the Author

About PE4life

PE4life is a national nonprofit advocacy organization committed to inspiring active, healthy lifestyles in children and youth through health-related school physical education programs. PE4life programs meet the needs of all students; use the latest technology, which enables individual assessments and monitoring of progress toward personalized goals; and positively emphasize the importance of physical activity and fitness in ways that students can benefit from their entire lives.

PE4life has achieved success through a realistic and flexible model that can fit into community school systems and local recreation programs. Driven by education, advocacy, and community partnerships, the PE4life model is an evidence-based working solution to the physical inactivity and childhood obesity epidemic in the United States.

About Phil Lawler

Phil Lawler is a retired physical education teacher who spent most of his career at Madison Junior High in Naperville, Illinois, and is the PE4life director of instruction and outreach. He taught physical education for 34 years and has served as the director of the PE4life Academy in Illinois since 2001. During the Academy's first three years, he trained nearly 700 physical educators, school administrators, and community leaders. The PE4life program at Madison Junior High has been featured in the *Wall Street Journal, USA Today, Time, Newsweek, US News & World Report,* the *Washington Post,* PBS, CBS News, and other media.

More than 150 school districts across the United States have visited the PE4life Academy at Madison Junior High since 1998 to learn about the school's New Physical Education program. The Centers for Disease Control and Prevention in 1997 recognized the program as one of the six model PE programs in the United States.

Lawler was named Illinois Middle School Physical Education Teacher of the Year in 1999, the same year he was inducted into the Illinois High School Baseball Coaches' Hall of Fame. In 2002 Lawler was named to the *USA Today* First Team All-American Teaching Team—the first PE teacher to make first team.

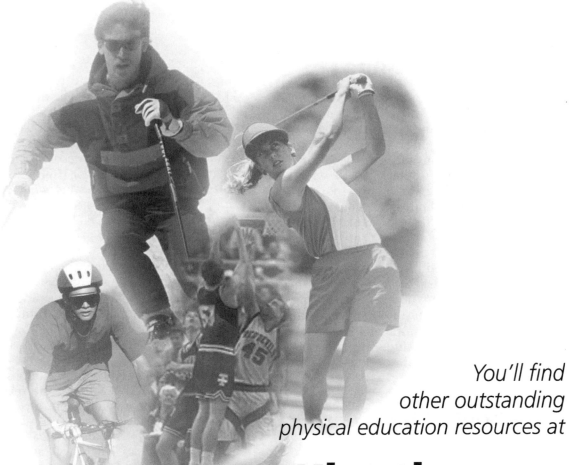